Photographer on an Army Mule

Chr. Barthelmess.

Photographer

Fort Keogh,

Montana.

PHOTOGRAPHER ON AN ARMY MULE

by *Maurice Frink*

with *Casey E. Barthelmess*

Foreword by *Robert M. Utley*

UNIVERSITY OF OKLAHOMA PRESS : NORMAN AND LONDON

By Maurice Frink

Cow Country Cavalcade (Denver, 1954)
When Grass Was King (With W. Turrentine Jackson and
Agnes Wright Spring) (Boulder, Colo., 1956)
Photographer on an Army Mule (With Casey E. Barthelmess)
(Norman, 1965)

Library of Congress Catalog Card Number: 65–24202
ISBN: 0–8061–2182–3

To
Toby and Edith
two patient wives

Foreword

by
Robert M. Utley

ORE THAN four decades have passed since I shared in the
events on Custer Hill described by Maurice Frink in the
introduction to this book. Throughout the winter of my senior
year in high school, I had importuned Major Luce, that stern
old veteran of the Seventh Cavalry who presided over the scene
of the last stand, to hire me as a summer "historical aide" at the
battlefield. In my youthful innocence, I did not understand how
absurd a proposition that was; if stationing a seventeen-year-old
on Custer Hill to tell the story to tourists did not betray faulty
judgment, it did contravene National Park Service regulations.
But the major could not find anyone else, and while his superiors
looked the other way, he took a chance.

When Maurice Frink and Casey Barthelmess came to Custer
Battlefield for that seventy-first anniversary gathering, I had
been on the job for one week of what was to extend over six
collegiate summers and turn me from a career in law to one in
history. I was drawn at once to Frink, for we were both from
Indiana. I was drawn to Casey Barthelmess too; aside from his
quiet warmth and complete lack of pretense, he represented a
link to the Indian-fighting army that had become my consuming
historical interest. I valued the friendship of both as long as
they lived.

The collaboration that flowed from the accord struck between
Frink and Barthelmess on that June day in 1947 resulted in
Photographer on an Army Mule. It is the story of Casey's father,
Christian Barthelmess, Bavarian immigrant, soldier, musician,
ethnologist, and, most notably, photographer of the western
scene during the closing decades of the nineteenth century. It

is also the story of Casey, pioneer cowman who made some history in his own right on the Montana range. It represents the culmination of Casey's lifelong quest for a means to preserve the works and memory of his father.

As bandsman and later chief musician of the Twenty-second and Second Infantry bands, Christian Barthelmess served in the U.S. Army from 1876 to 1903, in New Mexico, Arizona, Colorado, Montana, and Cuba. His most intimate association was with Fort Keogh, Montana. He was stationed there in 1890 when his close friend Lt. Edward W. Casey led his crack troop of Cheyenne Indian scouts off to South Dakota to participate in the Ghost Dance War, the last major Indian hostility. While trying to arrange peace talks with the Sioux leaders, Lieutenant Casey was shot and killed. The previous summer Christian Barthelmess had named his newborn son for the able and popular officer. In 1906, three years after his retirement, Christian Barthelmess was killed in the cave-in of a ditch at Fort Keogh. His son Casey spent his life as a cowman not far from the place of his birth.

Beyond a service record, the memory of his son, and two ethnological articles in a German-language newspaper, Christian Barthelmess left little documentation to support a biography. Far more important, he did leave a priceless collection of photographs accumulated over a period of three decades of military travels. They were carefully preserved by his son for the time when they could be laid before the public. This book reproduces more than a hundred of them, most for the first time. Principally they comprise military and Indian scenes and portraits taken in the Southwest and Montana. The Indian portraits reveal a notable sensitivity to Indian character and form Barthelmess's most significant contribution to the western record. Particularly is this true of his photographs of the Northern Cheyennes, among whom he lived and worked for so long at Fort Keogh and with whom he formed intimate friendships.

I applauded this book when it was first published in 1965, and I greet with equal acclaim the decision of the University of Oklahoma Press to bring it back into print. In a literal sense, I

Foreword

was "present at the creation" of *Photographer on an Army Mule.* Aside from the personal perspective, I regard it as a valuable and fascinating view of the frontier in its closing years, a volume that merits the notice of anyone interested in America's westward movement.

Acknowledgments

So MANY librarians, historians, writers, and other friends helped me with this book that to list all would be impractical. I hope they know they have my thanks.

I am particularly indebted to Harry H. Anderson of Milwaukee, Willena D. Cartwright of Denver, and John D. Mitchell of Boulder, Colorado, who read the manuscript and in many instances saved me from myself.

Parts of the manuscript were read (and are the better for it) by Mari Sandoz, New York, the Reverend Father Peter J. Powell, Chicago, and Mrs. Evelyn Dahl, Santa Fe.

Others who helped in one way or another include Bruce T. Ellis and Franklin G. Smith, Santa Fe; Margaret W. (Mrs. William S.) Jackson, Denver; Robert M. Utley, Washington, D.C.; Don Russell, James S. Gray, and Colton Storm (Newberry Library), Chicago; Mary Jane Bragg, Los Angeles; Wallace S. Wiggins, Whittier, California; John Artichoker, Jr., Lame Deer, Montana; Bob White, Rocky Boy's Agency, Box Elder, Montana; Father Emmett, St. Labre Mission, Ashland, Montana; Don Hollowbreast, Birney, Montana; Fred Mazzulla, Denver; Dale F. Giese, Fort Union National Monument, New Mexico; and Don Rickey, St. Louis, Missouri.

Colonel Raymond C. Ball, chief of the Historical Services Division, Department of the Army, Washington; Victor Gondos, Jr., and Elmer O. Parker, National Archives and Records Service, Washington; and Joseph M. O'Donnell, chief, Archives and History Division, West Point, were, it seemed to me, interested and helpful beyond the call of duty.

My greatest debt, of course, is to Casey E. Barthelmess of

Miles City, Montana, for entrusting to me the telling of his father's story.

None of the help I had from these or others lessens my responsibility for errors.

MAURICE FRINK

Boulder, Colorado
June, 1965

Son of the Picture Man

I FIRST HEARD of the soldier-musician-photographer Christian Barthelmess from his rancher son, Casey, on June 25, 1947, at the Little Big Horn battlefield in southeastern Montana. There, on that seventy-first anniversary of the day when "Custer died to the trumpet," Major Edward S. Luce, now deceased, then superintendent of Custer Battlefield National Monument, had assembled a group of history-minded friends for a tour of the area and a new discussion of old mysteries that still surround that tragic fight between the soldiers and the Sioux and Cheyennes. I had driven from my home in Indiana to be there. Others present were Robert M. Utley, a seasonal aide on the battlefield, then still in high school, now chief historian, National Park Service, Washington, D.C.; the late Charles Kuhlman of Polytechnic, Montana, author of *Legend into History*; the late Dennis Moran of Lake Andes, South Dakota, who had served in 1880–81 with an Eleventh Infantry detachment of Sioux Indian scouts; D. L. Egnew of Hardin, Montana; George G. Osten of Billings—and this rancher, Casey E. Barthelmess, who with his young son Randall had driven over from the family ranch on Mizpah Creek, Custer County, Montana.

We spent the day going over the battlefield. Everyone except me had been there many times. That evening, after Evelyn Luce, the Major's wife, had fed us and we were sitting on the shaded porch of the superintendent's house, Casey Barthelmess quietly pushed back his chair and remarked that he was going for a little walk. A hunch made me follow him.

Casey led the way into the National Cemetery that forms part of the federal area. White headstones in rows as straight as ranks of a military formation mark the burial places of men killed in the Indian wars of the West, their lonely lines reinforced in later years by soldiers slain in more recent conflicts.

As we passed the graves, I noted the names of officers and men I had read about, and also many stones marked only with a number and the familiar words:

Unknown Soldier

We passed a large monument "To the Officers and Soldiers Killed or Who Died of Wounds Received in Action in the Territory of Montana, While Clearing the District of the Yellowstone of Hostile Indians." I saw a white stone slab inscribed simply:

Chippewa

Indian

Woman

and a larger one, to

White Swan

U. S. Scout With Reno

Died Aug. 12, 1904, Aged 53 Yrs.

We paused briefly at a headstone whose inscription paid tribute to one whose service was of a humbler kind:

Margaret J. wife of Amos W. Littlejohn

Dau of D. & M. Caton of Owen Co Ind

Died Oct 5 1872 Ae. 36 Yrs 4 Mos 5 Ds

Laundress of Co I 6 Inft

Grave No. 126

We walked down one of the grassy aisles between graves, the aisle that runs from the central flagstaff westward toward the

Little Big Horn River, and stopped in front of the nineteenth marker in the eighth row of that section. There I read:

Christian

Barthelmess

Chief Mus

2 Inf Band

April 10, 1906

"My father's grave," Casey said; and he added, after a moment: "He was first buried at Old Fort Keogh, Montana, where he died and where I was born. When the army abandoned Keogh, in 1908, he and the others buried there were brought here." Then Casey told me a little about his father's life as a soldier, and added: "He was a photographer, too. Some time maybe I can show you some of the pictures he took."

But I started back to Indiana the next day, and four years passed before I saw any Barthelmess pictures. After I had moved west, Casey came to visit me in Colorado, bringing a box of old photographs. They were sepia prints, the familiar type of the Victorian era, on dog-eared and time-stained card mounts—but these pictures were vibrant with people and places: Indians and Indian camps, troopers and army posts, ferryboats, roundup wagons, military maneuvers and scouts in the field. "I have more at home," said Casey. "I just brought a few, to give you an idea. Many of Dad's pictures are in the National Archives, too."

As he talked about the man who had taken the photographs, I was touched by Casey's quiet pride in his father, but beyond that I was stirred by the feeling that Chief Musician Christian Barthelmess had been an unusual soldier, a man whose contribution to the recorded history of the West had been overlooked. From that day, I wanted to put the man and his work, pictorial and printed, into the record where they belong, both in justice to him and because of their interest and value to others.

"There ought to be a book about your father," I remember saying to Casey.

And here at last is that book, which had its inception on that June day in 1947 at Custer Battlefield when I first met the Keogh-born rancher known to his father's old Cheyenne Indian friends as "Son of the Picture Man."

The book is about Christian Barthelmess, but some of it has to be about Casey, too; for the collection of photographs on which it is based would not exist had not Casey preserved those pictures that were left in the family's possession, persevered in finding others, and succeeded in identifying some that his father had left unidentified. Casey kept the grass from growing over his father's tracks. He is himself a living part of the West his father knew. Because of these things, and because so much in the book has come from Casey, it seems important for the reader to know him first.

Casey E. Barthelmess could never be mistaken for anything but what he so eloquently is—bronco rider, cowboy, and rancher of the old school, from saddle-bent legs to wind-seamed, sun-burned face. His walk is that of a man who belongs on a horse. His speech is sprinkled with cowboyisms: "We was just shackin' along. . . . the bronc broke in two and turned it on. . . . history sure is holdin'. . . . goin' down the creek [meaning home]." Casey bears scars on his hand and arm to remind him of the day when, as a boy, he was attacked by a supposedly tamed coyote that broke away from a chain leash. His eyes are narrow slits that sometimes sparkle and now and then grow misty as he talks of his days on the open range as horse wrangler, bronco rider, and cowpuncher, and, before that, as a boy at historic Fort Keogh.

That United States Army post on the Yellowstone River, at the mouth of the Tongue, was built and garrisoned by Colonel Nelson A. Miles and the Fifth Infantry in 1877, following the construction of a cantonment two miles east in the fall of 1876. Casey was born July 18, 1890, while his father was stationed at Fort Keogh with the Twenty-second Infantry. The boy was named after a lieutenant of that regiment, Edward W. Casey. Young Barthelmess was a daily spectator at a real-life pageant in which the actors were the soldiers, scouts, buffalo hunters, mule skinners, Indians, and cowboys, and the panoramic back-

xvi

ground was the Northern Pacific Railway stockyards, the near-by cowtown, Miles City, the rivers, and the gray cliffs, the camel-back hills and the great wide plains beyond. A fondness for animals and for the men who worked with them was bred in him, as with a boy's impressionable eyes he took in all that went on around him in that heartland of horse and cow country.

In 1901, when he was eleven, Casey joggled on a freight wagon over the old Fort Buford and Camp Poplar road, still dotted with the whitened skulls and bones of buffalo, to the Colgan ranch on the Missouri, 150 miles north of Keogh. There through the summer he "chored for his keep." The next two summers and one winter he worked on the Mothershead ranch, sixty miles south of the Missouri on the XIT range. From cow-hands who had brought Longhorn herds up the trail from Texas, he began to learn the fundamentals of handling livestock.

There were seven children (one had died) in the Barthelmess family when Christian Barthelmess was killed. Casey was then fifteen. He and two of the other children stopped school and went to work to support themselves and help the rest of the fatherless family. Casey found a job working with horses for the LO Ranch on Mizpah Creek, a tributary of the Powder River. The LO had been established in 1881 by John M. Holt, a historic figure in the Montana cattle industry. In its heyday it ran at times fifteen thousand head or more on open range extending far beyond the hundred thousand acres comprising the ranch proper. In Casey's day, the LO roundup wagon, with others from neighboring outfits, worked the range between the Tongue and the Box Elder. There were line camps at Chalk Buttes and on the Box Elder, and a horse camp at the head of Timber Creek.

"The LO had several hundred stock horses," Casey recalls, "and my first spring there I felt fortunate when, much to my liking, I was assigned a job in the horse department. I worked with and under Charles Westley, a splendid horse man. It was a fine break for a young 'pistol' like me to have him for a teacher. When the roundup wagon started to work in May, my second year at the LO, I was given the job of horse wrangler. The days were long, but interesting and exciting, and I had the opportunity to learn more about handling stock, especially horses, and about the men who did the work. I became interested in breaking horses, an occupation I continued for many years at the LO. Occasionally I took part in rodeos, and this paid off; the money I won proved most useful in my getting started in ranching on my own."

During winters on the LO, whenever he could, young Casey studied schoolbooks that Mrs. Holt gave him. And whenever he could, he drew pictures of cowboys and horses. One winter he spent on the WL Ranch, which was part of the LO, and this enabled him to attend a short term of school at Powderville, two and one-half miles away. He broke two young broncos that winter by riding them to school and back.

In 1909 he decided to be an artist, quit his job, went to Chicago, and enrolled for the winter in an art school. He took along some reproductions of lively western scenes by Charles M. Russell and told his instructor, "This is the kind of art I want you to teach me." The instructor said Russell's colors were exaggerated and his composition bad. He was so critical of the work of the cowboy artist that before long the Barthelmess boy transferred to a school in St. Paul. Soon after that, necessity brought him home, and he went back to work for the LO, attending business college at Miles City the next three winters.

He took part in his first rodeo in 1914—the Miles City Fourth of July Roundup—as pick-up man for the bronc riders. The next year he entered the main events himself—and won the bareback-riding championship of the Northwest on a horse named Bluejay. The horse bucked viciously, blindly hitting the arena fence, where he floundered and fell backward. Casey fell with the horse but stayed on, and when Bluejay got up Casey was still on top and finished out the ride.

Casey has traveled, but he has sojourned long or far from Montana only twice. Once was the period in the middle western art schools; the other time was during World War I, when he spent fifteen months in service. He volunteered in December, 1917, and asked to be assigned to the cavalry, of which the army at that time still had a dwindling force. At Fort Sam Houston, Texas, by a coincidence that pleased him, he was assigned to the same regiment that his father had joined in 1876 in Arizona— the Sixth Cavalry. Here he found some old friends, men he had known in 1903–1906 at Fort Keogh as members of Troops M, I, L, and K—the "Milk Squadron."

Casey's army experience included participation in an impromptu rodeo and field day celebration in France, where he showed the populace and a lot of military men, including some French officers, how a cowboy rode bucking horses bareback. His horsemanship relieved him of considerable drill in equitation, but ironically, when he was discharged at Camp Merritt, Long Island, on Easter Sunday, 1919, his final papers, through an army mistake, bore the notation: "Horsemanship: *None*."[1]

Back in Montana, Casey finished out the spring as a rider for the LO. That was a drought year in Montana, so range work was light, and after the Fourth of July Roundup at Miles City, Casey helped stage rodeos in South Dakota and competed in others. At the Miles City Roundup that year Casey contributed to the festivities what an authority on the subject has called "one of the greatest rides ever made."[2] This was on a horse named Skyrocket. As Casey tells it:

> I wasn't the only one who ever rode Skyrocket. At least five others did it, too. But I was the last one. He was a proud horse, a big bay, well bred and intelligent. The day I rode him, Colie Ward, another LO bronc peeler, eared him down for me in front of the grandstand, where he was blindfolded and saddled. That year, chutes were used for the first time at Miles, but as Skyrocket was the feature horse of the three-day rodeo, he had to be saddled and mounted in front of the grandstand. When they pulled off the

---

[1] Casey forgave the army for this, in light of another document—a letter written on February 13, 1919, by Captain John J. Bohn, Sixth Cavalry, Remount Depot No. 22, A.E.F., France: "I have personally known Corporal Casey E. Barthelmess 1003954 since December, 1917, during which period he has served under me in Troop H, Sixth Cavalry. Although not an old soldier, he was made a non-commissioned officer because of his steadiness, sound judgment and application to duty. He is in my opinion an absolutely trustworthy, courageous and efficient soldier."

[2] F. H. Sinclair (Neckyoke Jones), "Top Hands and Top Horses," *Montana Farmer-Stockman* (Great Falls), August 1, 1952.

blindfold and turned him loose, Skyrocket knocked Ward down and jumped over him. Then he tried to get rid of me, but I finished the ride and was much relieved when the whistle blew. Skyrocket was used for the last time the following year, and threw the man who tried to ride him. The horse was turned to pasture that winter; he never showed up in the spring.

Casey won $1,150 as a contest rider in 1919—"the most money I had ever seen at one time up to then. It wasn't gravy, either. That money didn't come easy. Bronco busting was a rough and rugged way to make a living. Competitors were real bronc riders right off the range—Rufus Rollen, Pat Loney, Bob Askins, Shorty Davis, Howard Tegland, and the Coleman boys, to name a few. And we rode reputation horses that needed no flank riggin' to make 'em buck—real performers, like Skyrocket, Whitesides, Limber Jim, and Powder River Gray."

In 1920, his rodeo winnings a-jingle in his pockets, Casey bought three of his favorite horses—Dutch, Chub, and Frying Pan—from the string he had ridden at the LO, quit his job there, acquired a team of work horses and a few cows, and began life as a rancher on a homestead he had taken up in 1913 on the Mizpah. There was a schoolma'am near, named Anna Oby, who was called Toby. In 1921 she married the cowboy. Casey and Toby have reared six children, who went to grade school at Cactus Patch, not far from the ranch, and then to high school in Miles City.[3]

As a rancher, Casey was first on the Mizpah to ditch run-off

[3] The children are Richard Christian Barthelmess, San Jose, California; Robert Garrison Barthelmess, Powderville Stage, Montana; Casey Edward Barthelmess, Los Angeles; Rosemary (Mrs. George Zettler), Los Angeles; Leo Frederick Barthelmess, Malta, Montana; and Randall A. Barthelmess, M.D., Washington, D.C. Two of the sons are Montana ranchers—giving point to a passage in Robert H. Fletcher's *Free Grass to Fences: The Montana Cattle Range Story* (p. 232): "Head south again over the billowing benchland and reach that jaunty, ever-vibrant hub of Montana's southeastern cowland, Miles City on the Tongue and Yellowstone. Here the tradition of trailherds and roundups is preserved and revered by the descendants of the old-he-ones—the first Terrett, Simpson, Holt, Barthelmess, Brown, Brewster, Spear, and other stalwarts who helped found and hold together the Montana Stockgrowers Association." Robert Garrison Barthelmess was president of the five-thousand-member Association, 1963–65.

water onto the sagebrush flats to make the land grow alfalfa.[4] Thus over the years the homestead grew into a profitable hay and Hereford ranch. In 1951 and 1952 Casey was president of the South-Eastern Montana Livestock Association. In 1954 he was designated Montana's Rancher of the Year, at the twenty-first Little International Livestock Exposition, by the Agricultural Club of Montana State College at Bozeman.[5]

When retirement time came, Casey and Toby moved to Miles City. There they live only about two miles from his childhood home on the old army post. In 1959, Casey was appointed a trustee of the Montana Historical Society. As release from ranching routine made it possible, he began retracing his father's footsteps, visiting sites of the southwestern outposts where Christian Barthelmess had been stationed before going with his regiment to Fort Keogh, hunting out some of the remote areas that the soldier-musician had photographed, and seeking persons who had knowledge of him and his work. What Casey learned about his father's early years, what he remembers about the later ones, and the results of his research in the National Archives and the Smithsonian Institution have gone into this book.

Casey dwells within half a day's drive of Custer Battlefield and its National Cemetery. I go back there with him now and then. Always, on entering the area, Casey walks first to the nineteenth granite headstone in the eighth row of the section that lies on the grassy slope between the flagstaff and the Little Big Horn, to salute in silence his soldier father.

[4] Casey E. Barthelmess, "Making the Flood Water Raise Crops," *Montana Farmer-Stockman*, July 1, 1933.
[5] *Montana State College Farmer*, Bozeman, June, 1954, p. 21.

Contents

Illustrations

Illustrations

xxvii

Photographer on an Army Mule

ONE

Journey from Bavaria

A LERT, OBSERVANT, with an ear for music, an eye for pictures, and a way with words, Bavarian-born Christian Barthelmess[1] migrated in his youth to America, in rebellion against compulsory peacetime military service in his fatherland—and then spent the best part of his life serving the armed forces of his adopted country. He was a man of convictions—obviously he believed in the right to choose. He was a good soldier, a musician of talent, something of a scholar, and an artist with the camera.

His military service began in 1876 when he enlisted in the Sixth Cavalry, United States Regular Army. Subsequently he served in three old-line infantry regiments, the Thirteenth, Twenty-second, and Second. He soldiered at Forts Apache (Arizona), Wingate and Bayard (New Mexico), Lewis (Colorado), and Keogh (Montana). He served in Cuba, 1898–99, and in the Philippines, 1900–1903. All told, Barthlemess served four five-year and two three-year consecutive enlistments, plus seven months of a third. Foreign duty counting double, he had, upon retirement in 1903, an aggregate military service of thirty years, three months, and three days.

Grass grows high over some of the tracks he made, but the trail is plain enough to mark him as one whose creative instinct rose above surrounding and circumstance. A Montana writer has said of him that "by nature he gazed beyond his horizon."[2]

---

[1] Fort Union (New Mexico) records show that a German with a strikingly similar name—Christian Bartholomus—served in the U.S. Mounted Rifles at Fort Union, being discharged June 30, 1860, about a decade before Christian Barthelmess came to America.

[2] Lou F. Grill, "Pictures Taken by Christian Barthelmess Preserve Scenes of Indian Wars in Northwest," *Miles City Daily Star*, September 26, 1949, p. 2.

Certainly, as he went about his duties as a soldier, Barthelmess had a certain awareness of the importance of the time and place in which he lived, for he preserved, photographically and in writing, many meaningful fragments of America's military adventure on the western plains.

He was chief musician, Second Infantry, when he retired and returned as a civilian to his family at Fort Keogh, where, three years later, he was accidentally killed. To his family he left a legacy of poignant memories and a pioneer heritage, official records of commendation for his military service, some highly original descriptions (published and unpublished) of his experiences as a soldier—and a trunkful of photographs.

Barthelmess was born April 11, 1854, at a Bavarian town called Klingenberg, on the Main River, forty miles southeast of Frankfort. The town was chartered in 1276. Its people produced pottery, textiles, and good red wine. A castle stood on foundations built by the Romans about the time the Christian era dawned. For centuries Bavaria was ravaged by wars and torn by the dynastic ambitions of its rulers. In 1870 it became an integral part of the new German empire, but it reserved a larger measure of independence than did other constituent states. Bavaria was a country that could endow a perceptive young man with a sense of history and a love for a land of hills and streams— an affection easily transferred to the mountains and plains, even the deserts, of the American West where Barthelmess spent most of his life.

He reached New York in the early 1870's, and began working his way westward, pausing for a while with relatives at Ironton, Ohio. He worked for a time in a factory making sauerkraut. He was twenty-two years and six months old when he joined the army, fifty-two when an excavation in which he was working caved in and crushed out his life. Eight children had been born to him and the former Catherine Dorothea Hansen whom he married in 1886 at Silver City, New Mexico.[3] He was sandy

[3] Catherine was born April 9, 1863, in Schleswig-Holstein, then under Danish control. The children, in addition to one who died in infancy, include Leo E. Barthelmess, Houston, Texas; Mrs. Florence Dinwoodie, Fargo, North Dakota; Mrs. Sophia Kerrigan, Jackson, Mississippi; Fred J. Barthelmess, Missoula, Mon-

haired, with blue eyes, spectacles (the Navahos called him Glass Eye), and a beard which he periodically dispensed with for a while and then regrew. He weighed into the army in 1876 at 140 pounds, and he then stood five feet, six inches tall. Thirty years later he weighed the same but was an inch and three-quarters taller.

He loved his family, the army, his camera, and music, perhaps in that order, and he loved the western country and its people. He was dedicated to his self-appointed task of recording the look of that land and the life of its people. No one knows where or when he obtained the camera that he kept at hand until his dying day. After retirement, he supported his family with his photography, supplemented by day labor.

His military records show that he was frequently on detached service for photographic assignments. His equipment must have been meager. His camera (make unknown) has long since disappeared. In the field, he carried his glass plates in a haversack, taking most of his pictures outdoors. They cover a wide range of off-duty and social as well as military activities of the units in which he served, depicting the terrain covered and the Indians and other frontier personages encountered. Only in his last years did he enjoy the luxury of a studio of his own—he called it his gallery—in a frame structure at Fort Keogh. He had studio arrangements at his previous stations, but at Fort Keogh he built his own. He and his family lived at that fort in a frame house which their milk cow, Molly, sometimes entered by lifting the door latch with her stub horn, to drink from the tub under the washroom pump. In that house, too, as soon as he had children old enough to carry a tune, Barthelmess organized them—first into a trio, then into a quartet, and eventually into a quintet—enforcing discipline with a gentle rap from his viola bow if one of the younger members grew restive or hit a false note. Mrs. Barthelmess had too many household duties to permit her to join the group, but her children remember the soft voice in which she sang as she went about her work. Members of the family appear

tana; and Mrs. Adelaide Wellems, Mrs. Marie Elizabeth Smith, and Casey E. Barthelmess, all of Miles City.

in some of his pictures, Mrs. Barthelmess usually holding her latest baby, the other children clutching her skirts. The Barthelmess dog, Bob, got into so many of the pictures that he almost became a trademark. When Bob died, the family gave him a solemn burial and a headstone; the funeral was photographed with the Barthelmess camera, but with someone other than Barthelmess squeezing the bulb since he himself is in the picture.

An unusual man, this Christian Barthelmess, "an excellent soldier, either in garrison or field, a fine musician, an honest, industrious, intelligent and a sober man. He is also an excellent photographer. I commend him as fully capable for everything he should represent himself to be," wrote W. H. Kell, captain, Twenty-second Infantry, at Fort Keogh on June 4, 1891.[4] Barthelmess had studied music at Leipzig, in his youth, and was acquainted with German literature as well as some of the classics. English words he sometimes wrote as he probably pronounced them—"worts" for words, "where" for were, "troad" for throat—but his native language he used with skill. In the early 1880's he contributed two articles about the Navaho Indians to *Der Westen*, a German newspaper published in Chicago, and he left a manuscript deftly describing the start in 1887 of a military reconnaissance expedition of which he was a member. One translator of his German script commented that Barthelmess was a master of the German language, with flawless grammar and an impressive vocabulary. He was a reader, and a rememberer, for he brightened his writings with Latin phrases, Biblical references, and apt and scholarly allusions to matters outside the ken of the average soldier, such as the Seven Sages of Greece and the writings of German poets and dramatists. He closed a descriptive list of some of his photographs not with the "*Gott sei dank*" that might have been expected of him at the

---

[4] Letter in possession of Casey E. Barthelmess, who also has a letter signed "Charles H. Muir, Captain (lately Adjutant) Second Infantry, Major Thirty-eighth U.S. Volunteer Infantry, Powell Barracks, Paso Caballo, Cienfuegos, Cuba, September 22, 1899," reading: "Sergeant Chris Barthelmess, Band, Second Infantry, has been under my command and observation for the last eighteen months, including the Santiago campaign. He was always a faithful, reliable man, a good soldier, and is a man that I consider it safe to recommend for positions of trust."

conclusion of what apparently had been an onerous task, but with the Latin *"Finis coronat opus! Laus Deo!"* ("The end crowns the work! Praise God!")

Barthelmess served in the Southwest during the Apache campaigns of the 1880's, and was a friend and student of the Navahos. In Montana he was a frequent and welcome guest in the camps of the Northern Cheyennes, and they were often in his studio and home. He knew Frederic Remington and General Miles—he photographed Miles in council with the Cheyenne chiefs. He photographed Indian women with their children and their dogs, and he photographed William H. Taft as civil governor of the Philippines at Manila in 1901. He knew two pioneer American anthropologists, Frank H. Cushing and Washington Matthews, and explored prehistoric ruins with them. He contributed his observations, as well as photographs and a transcription of Indian music, to their studies of the Navahos and Zuñis. He translated some of Matthews' writing about the Navahos into German for publication in *Der Westen.*

One of Barthelmess' good friends was Lieutenant Edward Wanton Casey, the West Pointer from California who in 1889–90 transformed some fifty breechclout Cheyennes into a crack cavalry scout unit—L Troop of the Eighth. It was under Lieutenant Casey that Barthelmess served on the reconnaissance expedition in 1887 into the unmapped country between Fort Lewis and the Grand Canyon. After Lieutenant Casey's death in 1891 in South Dakota at the hands of a Sioux Indian, Christian Barthelmess characteristically performed a sentimental service for his late friend who was also his son's namesake. He delivered the horse which Casey had been riding when he was killed, to Miss Sophia Swain, of California, their colonel's daughter. She had counted Lieutenant Casey among her suitors, and the horse was purchased from his estate by her father.

What the men of the western frontier looked like in its closing decades, what they wore, details of their equipment and activities, their actions at ease and under stress, all these and the historic events in which these men were the dramatis personae, as well as their off-duty relaxations with their families and comrades, can be better comprehended today because of the presence among them of a few men like Barthelmess, catching shadows in black boxes.[5] The names of some other western photographers are better known than his, but his work has its place among the best. So long as the Smithsonian Institution, the Library of Congress, the National Archives, and the United States Signal Corps maintain their collections, the product of his skill and artistry will continue to enrich the research of historians, for some of his photographs are preserved there, as well as in other libraries and historical collections.

Some photographs are not under his name and others are incorrectly identified, as is the case with the work of many other photographers of the time and place. Barthelmess was a soldier subject to military routine, which for him included directing bands and training musicians. His picture-taking may have been a voluntarily added responsibility at first, but as his artistry became evident, photography was made the primary part of his assignment—not only his first interest but an important duty. Handling his bulky camera, glass plates, tripod, and black focusing cloth, and doing his own processing, he would have been hard pressed indeed to make and maintain complete records.[6] The same was true of others in his field.

Many of the early western photographers were horsebackers, riding with governmental or private expeditions, moving with

[5] "Shadow catcher" was a common Plains Indian term for a photographer. Mari Sandoz says (letter, April 7, 1964, to Maurice Frink): "It was the black and white quality of the photograph that alarmed the Indian, who believed that control of his shadow meant control of his destiny. Perhaps this rose from the menace of the enemy who crept upon him against the sunlight, as any stalker of animal or man would, and so stepped into his shadow. In my childhood, only a good friend dared step in the shadow of an old buffalo-hunter Indian. We were taught to go around behind white people, but with Indians we had to be careful about shadows." George Bird Grinnell, in *The Cheyenne Indians* (II, 94) says: "Years ago Indians commonly refused to be photographed, because they believed that when the picture was taken away the subject was taken away too, and the actual man would die. They regarded the photographic print as a man's shadow."

[6] The wet-plate process required that the glass plates be sensitized with collodion just before exposure and developed within ten minutes. This method was used from 1851 until 1879, when relatively fast dry plates came on the market. Flexible film was first used in 1884, and it was only after it appeared that mass production of cameras and film began. In Barthelmess' day, very few individuals owned cameras or made photographs.

Christian Barthelmess, aged 33, as a member of the Twenty-second Infantry at Fort Lewis, 1887.

Mrs. Christian Barthelmess at Keogh, 1890.

the frontier flux, and often losing, one way or another, such records as they did keep, as well as pictures themselves. Sometimes a roving cameraman threw in for a while with a sedentary one who could provide a studio for the processing of plates. Trading or selling of negatives and prints, and of the right to reproduce them, was not uncommon. Researchers have encountered frustrating difficulties in determining with certainty the origin of some photographs.

In December, 1904, the year after he retired from the army, Christian Barthelmess clearly identified several hundred of his pictures and mounted them in albums now in possession of his son, Casey. The old soldier did omit some dates and details that it would be good to have, but his son has been able to supply many of these. Christian Barthelmess wrote his picture identifications in a notebook in which he also recorded the fact that hundreds of his plates had been stolen or damaged while in storage when he was on foreign duty. The collection which he left has been amplified by the addition of many of his photographs found in libraries or in the hands of individuals.

Barthelmess usually affixed his photographic prints to cardboard mounts on which were imprinted his name and the name of the post where he was stationed. Sometimes he used his full name, sometimes he abbreviated Christian to "Christ," "Chris," "Ch." or just "C." Embellishing the printed name was a scroll-work device, varying in the degree of its ornamentation, but usually including a drawing of an artist's easel and palette and, in the case of some of his Fort Keogh photographs, a sketch of a box camera of the 1880's. One of his imprints bore the added notation: "Duplicates can be had at any time."

Deplorable as was the loss of many of his original plates, it is fortunate that so many of his pictures were preserved, to help later generations visualize a historic period that passed with the buffalo, the Indian, and the men and women of the frontier army posts.

TWO

Young Man in the Old Army

CHRISTIAN BARTHELMESS began his western adventure where countless others began theirs, at St. Louis, Missouri, for decades the main gateway to the new land beyond the river. There, on November 15, 1876, Barthelmess took the oath that made him a thirteen-dollars-a-month private in the United States regular army. He was sworn in by First Lieutenant William C. Forbush, Fifth Cavalry, and was assigned to E Troop of the Sixth Cavalry at Fort Apache, Arizona Territory.[1]

Barthelmess soldiered through a period when the nation's military fortunes ran low. One historian refers to the time from 1865 to 1880 as the "Dark Ages of the Regular Army."[2] The Civil War had preserved the Union but had left the government with military dangers to meet and only a shrunken force, poorly manned and inadequately equipped, with which to meet them. On the heels of Reconstruction in the South came a revival of the westward migration which the Civil War had slowed down. Migrants and settlers west of the Missouri clamored for protection against the Indians, to whom the national government had paid relatively little attention during the Rebellion. Withdrawal of federal troops from western stations to fight in the South had been to the Indians an indication of weakness and had increased the tempo of their resistance to encroachment on land they considered theirs. On the nation's southwestern border an insecure emperor ruled Mexico for Napoleon and was unfriendly to the

[1] Like many other army posts, this one was first called Camp Apache, the word "fort" coming into use later, much as the original use of "company" to designate a cavalry unit gave way to the word "troop." In this book the latter designation is used in both instances, except in direct quotations.

[2] William Addleman Ganoe, *The History of the United States Army*, 298–354.

United States. In Canada the Fenian movement, supporting Ireland's struggle for independence, stirred sympathetic Americans to an extent that embarrassed Washington in its relations with Great Britain, and the Louis Riel rebellion threatened the Canadian government and hence worried ours. The financial panic of 1873 added to the nation's troubles and increased the restlessness that stimulated the westward thrust.

Volunteer regiments that had won the war for the Union melted away afterward. The size of the regular army was increased for a time immediately after the Civil War, but in about a decade, despite reasons for maintaining a strong force, an economy wave lowered its strength. Among those in its ranks during this period were many good men, but a large proportion were there only because they had no place to go in civilian life or because they came "from the bottom of the economic ladder, or had fallen from an intermediate rung."[3] In the dull routine of garrison life some of these proved restless and undependable (drinking was widespread and especially damaging among the officers), although most of them displayed in action traits in keeping with the best—traits such as endurance under privation and courage under fire. Pay was low, food sometimes bad and always monotonous, equipment was often lacking, and among enlisted men desertions were so common as to be a major problem. Some officers—George A. Custer for one—dealt mercilessly with men they caught going over the hill. Custer himself was court-martialed in 1867 on several charges, including excessive cruelty and illegal conduct in ordering deserters shot. Custer, then a lieutenant colonel in the Seventh Cavalry serving on the Southern Plains, was convicted and given a year's suspension, although the sentence was remitted after ten months. He was considered as getting off lightly because of his Civil War record.[4]

In 1876, the regular army's authorized strength was 29,970, but only 28,150 men were in uniform. The cavalry could muster only 9,038 of its authorized 11,381. For the year 1877, Congress,

[3] Don Rickey, Jr., *Forty Miles a Day on Beans and Hay*, 18.

[4] Jay Monaghan, *Custer*, 298–303; Fred Dustin, *The Custer Tragedy*, 21; George Armstrong Custer, *My Life on the Plains*, 182–83.

by an act passed August 15, 1876, ordered the army further reduced to 25,000 men. There were then twenty-five regiments of
infantry, five of artillery, and ten of cavalry. Importance of the
mounted troops was recognized in the retrenchment act, which
specified that the cut in total strength be effected without re-
ducing the cavalry. Recruiting in general was suspended. The
law permitted re-enlistment of noncoms and of "old soldiers of
good character"; but only "the necessary mechanics and musicians," cavalry recruits, and Indian scouts were to be enlisted.[5]

The Inspector General of the army in 1876 put a good light on
affairs, nevertheless. His report for that year noted that the
diminished strength of the army had prevented an improvement
in the instruction of the troops, but added that "their discipline
is good and their efficiency satisfactory." To the army's everlast-
ing credit, history sustains him, for the record shows that on
widely scattered fronts in an intermittent war continuing more
than a quarter of a century the regular army encountered Indians in more than one thousand actions, from full-scale battles
to minor skirmishes, and that it suffered an average of only two
casualties (killed and wounded) for each action listed.[6]

The actions range from well-known battles involving large
numbers of men and high casualties to such obscure tragedies
as one in 1867 near Fort Reno, Dakota Territory, involving a
detachment of Company F, Twenty-seventh Infantry, in which
one enlisted man was "killed while herding." Many actions were
engaged in by small units, some only by Indian scouts or other
scouts attached to the military. Typical listings are "Attack on
stage," "Mail escort," "Wood choppers," "Indian attack on

[5] "Report of the General of the Army," W. T. Sherman, in Secretary of War,
Annual Report, 1876, I, 24, 25, 75, and Charts A and B following p. 40. Financial
results achieved by the retrenchment: War Department expenditures in 1873
were $46,323,138; in 1876 they were down to $38,070,889, and in 1880 to
$29,322,000. By 1890 they were up again, to $31,689,000. By comparison, in
1945 they were $49,688,628,000.

[6] The record covering this period is a 28-page report, prepared in 1891 and
entitled *Chronological List of Actions, &c., with Indians from January 1, 1866, to
January, 1891*. This list shows, in fourteen parallel columns, the dates and places
of each of the "*Actions, &c.*,"; the troops engaged and commanding officer;
officers, enlisted men, and citizens killed and wounded; Indians killed, wounded,
and captured; and the source of the information.

settlers," and "6th Inf., G, guard on steamers *Josephine* and *Benton*," on the Yellowstone River near its mouth in Montana, where one enlisted man was killed (August 23, 1876).

Tabulation of the Adjutant General's Office figures (they are not totaled in the printed report) shows 1,065 *"Actions, &c.,"* for the twenty-six-year period (January 1, 1866, through January 7, 1891).

KILLED		WOUNDED	
Officers	58	Officers	72
Enlisted men	874	Enlisted men	988
Total army killed	932	Total army	
Citizens	522	wounded	1,060
		Citizens	114

This averages a little less than one army man killed and just about one wounded, or approximately two casualties for each of the 1,065 engagements on the printed list.

Its own casualties the army probably reported fairly accurately, but losses sustained by Indians must have been to a great extent estimates and, except perhaps for those captured, must have involved guesswork. Being human, the officers on the scene quite possibly overestimated the damage they inflicted on a foe that was facile in quick removal of its slain and wounded from the field of combat. At any rate, the report gives these figures:

INDIANS

Killed	4,363
Wounded	1,143
Captured	10,384

As an example of the vagueness of statistics regarding Indian casualties reported by the army, the company return for an encounter at the Sierra Diablo, New Mexico, October 18, 1867, in which Companies D and K of the Third Cavalry had one enlisted man killed and six wounded, adds: "25 or 30 Indians killed or wounded."

In the year 1868 alone, soldiers fought Indians in 140 engagements recorded by the A.G.O.; in 1867, the number of *"Actions, &c.,"* was 126; in 1869, it was 115. On one single day in 1866 (October 3), Indians were engaged by army units in three separate states—Arizona, Colorado, and Nevada. The most famous battle—Custer's last—was only one of forty-one engagements in 1876. There was no year from 1866 to 1891 without at least one officially recorded encounter.

The A.G.O.'s *Chronological List* terminates with the Ghost Dance trouble with the South Dakota Sioux, which began late in 1890 and involved two actions in January of 1891. This is generally thought of as the last Indian war, but the last army engagement with Indians was not fought until 1898, at Leech Lake, Minnesota. There, from the fourth of October through the seventh, Chippewa Indians engaged in a fracas with detachments representing eight companies of the Third Infantry. One officer and six men were killed and fourteen wounded.

In addition to the A.G.O. *Chronological List of Actions, &c.,* there is a compilation in Francis B. Heitman's *Historical Register and Dictionary of the United States Army, 1789–1903.* Its title page designates it as "the unofficial work of a private compiler, purchased and published by direction of Congress." Heitman, an employee of the War Department for many years beginning in 1856 (he was born in 1838), carries his tabulation (II, 426–49) through 1898, listing fourteen engagements subsequent to the last one on the A.G.O. list. Adding these fourteen to the A.G.O. list of 1,065, plus one in 1865 involving the Fifth Infantry with Indians "near People's ranch, Arizona," gives a total of 1,080 actions. Heitman's own list, however, differs in many particulars from that of the A.G.O., and Heitman totals only 938 engagements, beginning in 1865 and running through 1898. Heitman omits detailed casualties, but says (II, 295) that in the "Indian wars, 1865–1898," the number of officers killed was 59, enlisted men, 860; officers wounded, 65, and men wounded, 960, making a total casualty list of 1,944.[7]

---

[7] *American Military History, 1607–1958* says, p. 278: "From 1865 to 1891, there were thirteen different campaigns and at least 1,067 engagements with the Indians." The same figure is used in *Army Information Digest,* 16. In *Winners of the West,* George W. Webb, editor of that periodical, published a "Chronological

"The whole story is a sad one," one army officer-historian says, and, he adds, it is

> by no means the proudest one in the country's history, but the Army had little to regret in it. The Army made no wars; as always, someone else made the wars, and the Army, coming in when all other agencies had lost control, ended them. . . . It was not uniformly successful, but even in defeat it made itself respected. The Indians gradually learned its point of view—that is, that a detachment might be beaten or even annihilated, but that the Army always kept coming, in as great strength as necessary, and ultimately won.[8]

The frontier troops fought with little public recognition or acknowledgment of their hardships and sacrifices and the injustices done them by bureaucratic inefficiency and corruption, Congressional apathy, or public neglect. The army went ahead and did its job, as "the cutting edge and holding power" of government and civilization, even though it was "in a very real sense physically and psychologically isolated from the rest of American life."[9] In this isolation, under circumstances sometimes not dissimilar to those endured by their forebears at Valley Forge, the frontier soldiers served their nation well. Many of our proudest military traditions today trace back to the Indian wars of the West, "while fighting still had banners and a sword."

So this was the army—the Old Army, some have fondly called it—when Christian Barthelmess became an American cavalryman. The branch in which he served his first enlistment was already doomed to extinction, though nobody knew this then. In the Indian wars, the regular army relied both on horsemen who sometimes fought on foot and on foot soldiers who sometimes mounted horses taken from the Indians. The painted warriors soon came to dread them both—the dogged "walk-a-heaps" and the dashing pony soldiers.

List of Indian War Battles," running serially from Vol. XIV, No. 1, to Vol. XV, No. 6, or from December 30, 1936, through June, 1938. The same list was later published in book form.

8 Oliver Lyman Spaulding, colonel, U.S. Field Artillery, *The United States Army in War and Peace*, 368.

9 Rickey, *Forty Miles a Day*, 349–50.

Mounted troops—the poet's "death on a lunging horse"— fought with America's forces in colonial days, and from that time on they carried with them an aura of romance inherited from the chivalric Middle Ages. The cavalry of the Civil and Indian wars evolved from the Dragoons, the Mounted Riflemen, and the Rangers of earlier decades. They provided swift mobility as a means of screening their own armies' movements, pursuing and demoralizing enemy retreats, breaking transport and communication lines, and striking suddenly at weak points or turning exposed flanks. On the plains, cavalrymen could meet the hit-and-run Indian warriors at their own game, although in a prolonged campaign the grain-fed mounts of the military were no match in speed and endurance for the grass-eating Indian ponies. Cavalry, usually dismounted, fought alongside the infantry in Cuba in 1898, and a few mounted units went to France in 1918, but mechanization began destroying the army horse before World War II. Conversion of cavalry regiments to tanks and trucks pulled the last of the old horse troopers' picket pins and launched the modernization that put into service the motorized war-making monsters of the armored cavalry.

It was a different world in 1876, when Recruit Barthelmess was ordered to Arizona—then a "dreaded and unknown land,"[10] six thousand miles or more from his native Klingenberg. Arizona had become a territory in 1863, though it did not attain statehood until 1912. In 1876 it contained a few scattered white settlements and about a dozen army posts. The Apache Indians and a rough border element kept the territory in turmoil. Military units took their stations in Arizona by long overland marches via New Mexico or by ships which reached Yuma from

[10] The phrase is Martha Summerhayes', in her *Vanished Arizona: Recollections of My Army Life*, 24. Mrs. Summerhayes' book is a charming account of a cultivated New Englander's experience as an officer's wife in the West. With her husband and the "Eighth Foot," as she called the infantry, she went from Fort D. A. Russell, Wyoming, to Camp Apache, Arizona Territory, in 1874, traveling by railroad to San Francisco and thence by steamship to Yuma. She was dismayed by the hardships but impressed by the men and the "straight backs and slim lines of those youthful figures! It seems to me any woman not an Egyptian mummy would feel her heart thrill and her blood tingle at the sight of them" (p. 265).

San Francisco by steaming down the west coast and then up the Gulf of California, a voyage of "only twenty days."[11]

Fort Apache, established in 1870 as a military post, was a key location in the Indian wars of 1872–73 and 1881–86. Official reports of the middle 1870's referred to it vaguely as being "in the White Mountain country." Colonel (Brevet Major General) A. V. Kautz, commander of the army's Department of Arizona with headquarters at Prescott, said, in a report dated September 15, 1876: "Camp Apache is being improved and having been wisely selected will be of use as long as there is apprehension of Indian trouble. It is isolated and difficult of access but it is as cheaply supplied as any other post in the territory."[12]

Strategically located on the northern edge of the San Carlos Apache reservation, in east central Arizona, Fort Apache sent troops out repeatedly against the Indians and was itself once attacked by them. Only after Geronimo's capitulation in 1886 did the post cease to play a significant role in frontier defense. In 1923 the Fort Apache buildings and grounds were turned over to the Department of the Interior for use by the Bureau of Indian Affairs as an Indian school. Many of the original buildings have been replaced by wooden structures, but a few storage facilities, living quarters, and the parade ground are still intact. One remaining building is said to have served as headquarters for General George Crook.[13]

When Christian Barthelmess entered the Sixth Cavalry, it was 108 men short of its authorized strength of 888. It was constituted as follows (authorized figures, in parentheses, precede actual figures): Privates (648), 570; officers (43), 43; sergeants (60), 53; corporals (48), 39; trumpeters (24), 20; farriers

11 Summerhayes, *Vanished Arizona*, 41.
12 Secretary of War, *Annual Report, 1876*, 102. The United States was then made up of three military divisions, which were geographical areas for administrative purposes, not brigade groupings (the regiment was the largest field unit). The divisions included *Pacific*, in which Arizona comprised one of three departments, the others being Columbia and California; *Atlantic*, including the eastern seaboard, Great Lakes states, and part of the South; and *Missouri*, which had five departments—Dakota, Platte, Missouri, Texas, and the Gulf. The Division of the Missouri extended from Illinois to Nevada and from Canada to the Gulf, taking in three-fourths of the Indian population. (*Ibid.*, 25, 439.)
13 National Park Service, *Soldier and Brave*, 166–67.

(horseshoers) and blacksmiths (24), 19; first sergeants (12), 12; saddlers (12), 12; wagoners (12), 7; sergeant major, quartermaster sergeant, chief musician, saddler sergeant, chief trumpeter, each (1), 1; total (888), 780.[14]

Each cavalry troop was also allowed one civilian veterinarian at $75 a month. Base pay of enlisted men was as follows: Private (including musician), $13; corporal, $15; sergeant, $17; first sergeant, saddler sergeant, chief trumpeter (cavalry), and principal musician (infantry), $22; quartermaster sergeant and sergeant major, $23.[15]

All the land forces of the military establishment were under command of a General of the Army, who from 1869 to 1883 was William Tecumseh Sherman. He drew $13,500 yearly. The annual salary of a colonel was $3,500; captain, mounted, $2,500; captain, not mounted, $1,800. The leader of the army band at the West Point Military Academy was paid $75 a month, the chief musician of a regiment, $60.[16]

In May, 1875, the Sixth Cavalry had come to Fort Apache, marching over the Santa Fe Trail, its regimental standard and troop guidons[17] shining in the sun and in the glory of its battle

[14] Secretary of War, *Annual Report, 1876*, Charts A and B following p. 40.

[15] War Department, *Regulations of the Army of the United States and General Orders in Force on the 17th of February, 1881*, 260. The base pay of $13 for a private was established in 1872 and continued until 1908, when it became $15. In 1917, with the advent of World War I, the rate became $30, and in 1922 it went back to $21. In 1940 it remained $21 for the first four months of service, after which it went to $30. When the army was first organized, in 1785, it was $4. (*The Army Almanac*, 697).

[16] *Regulations, 1881*. Soldiers re-enlisting drew longevity pay, an additional allowance of two dollars a month for the first re-enlistment, and another dollar a month for each successive and continuous re-enlistment thereafter. From their pay, twelve and one-half cents were deducted monthly for support of the Soldier's Home, to which a veteran might be admitted after "honest and faithful service of twenty years."

[17] Each regiment had a yellow-fringed blue silk standard, slightly larger than two feet square, with the regiment's number on a scroll beneath the eagle of the national arms. The standard was borne on a nine-foot lance. (*Regulations, 1881*, 284). The regimental standard, not the national flag, was carried into battle. The motto adopted by the Sixth Cavalry veteran association was "Fairfield," after a disastrous Civil War engagement in which the Sixth lost "all but honor and the regimental standard" (W. H. Carter, *From Yorktown to Santiago with the Sixth U.S. Cavalry*, 7). Guidons were swallow-tailed in shape, "with stars and stripes like the national flag," bearing the troop letter in yellow on a white stripe (*Regulations, 1881*, 284). Later the cavalry guidon was simplified to red

record—fifty-three engagements in three years of the Civil War, from the siege of Yorktown in 1862 to Appomattox in 1865, followed by ten years on the Kansas, Indian Territory, and Texas frontiers, fighting Indians, guarding courts, protecting cattle drives, and preventing ruffians from running unrestrained through counties where law and order were still to be established.[18]

Indians were only a part of the problems the military of that decade dealt with. Settlers "pushing into Kansas far beyond the safety line, and daring and unprincipled buffalo hunters, were constantly endangering the peace of the community at this period," by inciting the already aroused Indians to renewed depredations.

> Officers and men also found themselves confronted with all the hatred and bitterness left by the Civil War in the hearts of many persons, who had not been called upon to suffer as had those in some of the southern states. Many of the ex-Confederate soldiers had succumbed to the inevitable with bad grace, and the more lawless of them encouraged a hostile feeling toward the soldiers, who daily risked their lives to protect the settlements. It was enough to contend against the Indians, but when, by ill-treatment and assassination of comrades, the men were finally made to recognize the contempt in which the community held them, there was short shrift for the lawless guerrillas who were frequently encountered.[19]

The mission of the Sixth Cavalry in Arizona was to relieve the Fifth Cavalry, which had served there two years. The tour of duty in the Southwest begun by the Sixth in 1875 continued till the regiment went to South Dakota to help quell the Ghost Dance uprising in 1890. In the Southwest the Sixth participated

and white, without the stars and stripes. Guidons were so called because they marked the guide on which a formation was based.

[18] The Sixth went to Texas from New York via New Orleans on the steamship *Herman Livingston* in October, 1865. "One of the sad incidents of this trying voyage was the loss of horses thrown overboard to lighten the ship" during a storm off Cape Hatteras (Carter, *Yorktown to Santiago*, 134).

[19] *Ibid.*, 157–59. Spaulding, *The U.S. Army*, 370, says that a band of 250 armed desperadoes terrorized parts of New Mexico, 1877–80; upon being ordered by a sheriff to disband and return to their homes and ordinary vocations, they replied, "We have no homes; we are at our ordinary vocations."

in thirty-one recorded engagements with the Indians; in Texas, Kansas, and Indian Territory it had taken part, between 1867 and 1875, in twenty-nine. Army records show that between January 1, 1866, and May, 1875, when the Sixth came to Arizona, 217 fights had occurred between troops and Indians within the territory. The number of attacks by Indians upon ranches, wagon trains, stagecoaches, and travelers can only be conjectured.[20]

The Apaches, in this era of their transition from unrestricted freedom to the regimentation of reservation life, subjected Arizona and New Mexico, as well as Mexican states across the international boundary, to a state of intermittent conflict which might have compelled abandonment of that frontier had not the undermanned units of the regular army relentlessly pursued and harassed the Indians into submission. It was a long, hard war. Lieutenant Colonel W. H. Carter, in his history of the Sixth Cavalry, quotes one of the old officers of the regiment as saying:

> I am of the opinion that such services involved greater hardship, privation, endurance, more unremitting and unceasing vigilance, and more harassing difficulties of the march, and generally for longer periods of time, than any service experienced by me during the Civil War, with the possible exception of the Gettysburg campaign; this, too, with the chance of irretrievable disaster immeasurably greater, and the hopes of reward infinitely less.[21]

The reward that the Sixth Cavalry drew, after seven years in the thick of it in Arizona, was three years more of it in New Mexico and Colorado. The regiment exchanged stations with the Fourth Cavalry in 1883. Headquarters of the Sixth was established at Fort Bayard, New Mexico, some troops going to Forts Wingate, Stanton, and Cummings (New Mexico), and Fort Lewis (Colorado). At these stations, the men settled down for a time to garrison life, construction of quarters, installation of water systems, and general improvement of the posts, but this was interrupted in 1885 by the new Apache outbreaks which

[21] *Yorktown to Santiago*, 250.
[20] Carter, *Yorktown to Santiago*, 177, 179, 277.

called all troops into the field. There was another arduous campaign, during which General Miles replaced General Crook in command, and the next year the final Apache capitulation was achieved.

In this milieu, while still a stranger in a strange land,[22] young Christian Barthelmess spent his first five years in the army. He began taking photographs, and his musicianship put him into the regimental band and put three stripes on his arm. His own record of that first enlistment he wrote on the back pages of his *Soldier's Hand-Book*, now in possession of his son Casey:

> Enlisted 15 Nov 1876 by Lnt Forebush at St. Louis. Send to 6th Cav Dez 17, 1877. Prom. L. [lance] Sergt Aug 8th, 1878. Appointed act. 1st Sergt & Drum Major Dez 30, 1878. Relieved from duty as act. 1st Sergt & Drum Major May 2, 1879. Appointed L. Serg. July 5th, 1881. Transferred to Troop E, 6th Cav. Nov. 7, 1881. Appointed corpl. of E Troop, 6th Cav., Nov. 8, 1881. Discharged Nov. 14, 1881, at Ft. Apache, A.T.

If Barthelmess had not been a good soldier, it could not have been for lack of printed advice and instruction in his dog-eared *Hand-Book*. Whether one of those shirt-pocket-size government-issue paperbacks ever turned an enemy bullet, as some say an occasional pocket Bible did, is not of record, but that *Hand-Book*, carefully read and conscientiously heeded, could have kept many a soldier out of trouble. The book said that all "inferiors" (that is, enlisted men) were required to "obey strictly, and to execute with alacrity and good faith, the lawful orders of the superiors appointed over them." Superiors were charged with firmness in using their authority, "but with kindness and justice to inferiors." Punishment by flogging, branding, marking, or tattooing was no longer allowed, as it once had been, and superiors were forbidden to "injure those under them by tyrannical or capricious conduct, or by abusive language." Health rules included a warning against "inattention to na-

---

[22] Men from other lands, especially Germany and Ireland, entered the U.S. Army in large numbers during the period of the Indian wars. In 1884, of 8,775 men recruited in a year, 3,543 were foreign born (Secretary of War, *Annual Report, 1884*, 56).

ture's calls as a frequent source of sickness." On post or in camp, soldiers were to use only "the regularly established sinks." These, like the shambles where cattle were slaughtered for the mess tables, were not to be "allowed to become offensive." Men were not to go more than a mile from camp without permission, or to "lie out of quarters." They were advised to eat at regular hours but to "eat and drink as little as possible whilst marching." Rule Nineteen said:

> *Fire Low.*—A bullet through the abdomen (belly or stomach) is more certainly fatal than if aimed at the head or heart; for in the latter cases the ball is often glanced off by the bone, or follows round it under the skin. But when it enters the stomach or bowels, from any direction, death is inevitable, but scarcely ever instantaneous. Generally the person lives a day or two, with perfect clearness of intellect, often not suffering greatly. The practical bearing of this statement in reference to the future is clear. *Fire Low.*

Barthelmess' *Hand-Book* was dated 1884, and was based upon army regulations of 1881. Back of it was the full force of the Adjutant General (R. C. Drum), who directed its preparation; the Secretary of War (Robert T. Lincoln), who approved it; and the General of the Army (Phil Sheridan), by whose command it was issued—with a cautionary note to the effect that any soldier who lost his *Hand-Book* would be charged forty-five cents.

The Sixth Cavalry had a band from its earliest years of service. In Barthelmess' day, the applicable regulation provided:

> When it is desired to have bands of music for regiments there will be allowed, for each, sixteen privates to act as musicians, in addition to the chief musicians authorized by law, provided the total number of privates in the regiment, including the band, does not exceed the legal standard. Regimental commanders will designate the proportion to be subtracted from each company for a band. The musicians of the band will, for the time being, be dropped from the company muster, but they will be instructed as soldiers, and liable to serve in the ranks on any occasion. They will be mustered in a separate squad under the chief musician, with the non-commissioned staff, and be included in the aggregate in all regi-

mental returns. When a regiment occupies several stations, the band will be kept at the headquarters, provided troops be serving there.[23]

Members of the band wore the regulation regimental uniforms plus such ornaments or insignia as the commanding officer deemed suitable. Cavalry bands were usually mounted on white or gray horses.

"Bands of music" have been a part of the American army since the days when fifers and drummers, led by fifer-majors and drummer-majors as they were then called, accompanied General George Washington's troops into battle against the British—and serenaded General Washington at Valley Forge on February 22, 1778, his forty-sixth birthday. In those days the drummers sounded the military calls, as buglers did in later times. The transition to brass bands, patterned on the European style which had been set by Germany, came about gradually, as the early, imperfect construction of brass wind instruments was improved. The history of the Marine Corps band and the Military Academy band at West Point goes back to the early 1800's. Army regulations in 1834 allowed infantry regiments to organize bands of ten musicians, and established the position of chief musician (leader); in 1845 the strength was increased to sixteen men. There were bands with United States forces in the Mexican War, and music became an increasingly important part of the army in 1861, when the North organized its forces for the Civil War. Many Union units maintained complete bands; during field operations the musicians sometimes laid aside their instruments and attended the wounded or carried water or ammunition. A conspicuous exception occurred on April 1, 1865, when General Philip H. Sheridan kept his band performing under heavy fire at Five Forks, "playing Foster's 'Nelly Bly' as cheerily as if the battle was a country picnic." In the Spanish-American War, almost every regiment had its band. General Pershing took an interest in raising the quality of army music in World War I, and brought about an increase in the size of bands

[23] *Regulations, 1881*, 23.

and the training of band leaders. In World War II, bands played for American fighting units on many fronts.[24]

During the Indian wars in the West, functions of the regimental band were to play at parades and other formations and at guard mount and retreat, to send outgoing forces into the field with martial music in their ears, and to welcome troops returning to their posts. There were occasional post concerts and, for the band members, continual practice and instruction.

Among Indian fighters, Custer, like Sheridan, made much use of his band. He kept it playing so continuously, on post and in the field, that one of his men, returning from a campaign, reported being fed on "one hardtack a day and 'The Arkansas Traveler.' "[25] On the Southern Plains in 1868, Custer started a day's march with what amounted to a parade. The band, preceded only by the guides and scouts, led the troops out of camp to the tune of "The Girl I Left Behind Me." In one of his books Custer tells how he kept the music up front at the fighting climax of a winter campaign:

> Immediately in rear of my horse came the band, all mounted, and each with his instrument in readiness to begin playing the moment their leader, who rode at their head, and who kept his cornet to his lips, should receive the signal. . . . a single rifle shot rang sharp and clear on the far side of the Cheyenne village. . . . Quickly turning to the band leader, I directed him to give us the 'Garry Owen.' At once the rollicking notes of that familiar marching and fighting air sounded forth through the valley. . . . In this manner the battle of the Washita began [November 27, 1868].[26]

When the Thirteenth Infantry marched back to Fort Wingate after four years in the field along the border of Arizona and New Mexico, according to one of the men there, "the boys at the fort sure gave us a big blow out, and the band met us on the mountain and the music sure made our hearts glad."[27] Ganoe's *History of the United States Army*, (page 236), recalls that "the

[24] William Carter White, *A History of Military Music in America*, 29, 74ff.; *Army Almanac* (1950), 870–73; also, extract from AWC File No. 3595, Historical Services Division, Department of the Army.

[25] Monaghan, *Custer*, 330.

[26] *My Life on the Plains*, 219.

Commencement portrait of Edward Wanton Casey, in June, 1873, when he was graduated from West Point, commissioned a 2nd lieutenant, and posted to the Twenty-second Infantry, in which he served nearly eighteen years.

Bert Vaugh photograph

Rancher Casey Barthelmess at home on the Mizpah, 1940.

regimental band and four companies of the Twenty-first Infantry were present in 1869 at the driving of the golden spike, a few miles west of Ogden, when east and west were made into one [as the first United States transcontinental railroad line was completed with the junction of the Central Pacific and the Union Pacific]. It is said that the soldier musicians piped away lustily." Walt Whitman, in his *Leaves of Grass*, preserves his recollection of hearing "Italian Music in Dakota," as he entitled a poem dedicated to "The Seventeenth—the finest Regimental Band I ever heard."[28]

Christian Barthelmess left no record to show what the instrumentation of the Sixth Cavalry band was in 1876, but his son Casey recalls that around the turn of the century, when Chief Musician Barthelmess was in the Second Infantry band at Fort Keogh, the equiment included cornet, bass and alto horns, French horn, clarinet, piccolo, baritone, trombone, bass and snare drum, and tambourine. In earlier days, at similar posts, the instrumentation was less complete. Christian Barthelmess was adept with all the instruments, but he particularly liked the alto horn and the tuba, and, on special occasions, the French horn. It was his French horn and his viola—which he sometimes restrung so it could be used as a violin—that he was specially fond of playing at home.

When his first five-year enlistment expired, Christian Barthelmess was discharged, November 14, 1881, at Fort Apache. He was a civilian only overnight. On November 15, at the same post, he re-enlisted, this time in the infantry, at Fort Wingate, in the Navaho country of New Mexico. On November 25, he became a lance (temporary) corporal, and on December 6

27 Rickey, *Forty Miles a Day*, 76.
28 The late Fiorello H. La Guardia, congressman and mayor of New York City, was the son of an Italian immigrant who enlisted in the U.S. regular army in 1882 and became leader of the Eleventh Infantry band. In his autobiography, *The Making of an Insurgent*, La Guardia recalled his life as a child on army posts, particularly in Arizona. He wrote that his first awareness of political corruption came from observing the way in which Indians were robbed by "the small-fry ward heelers" serving political appointments as reservation agents, and from the fact that his father died in 1901 of illness incurred by eating diseased beef sold to the army during the Spanish-American War by dishonest contractors (pp. 22, 33).

was promoted to principal musician of the Thirteenth Infantry's regimental band, Fort Wingate. In this second enlistment, his life and works began to expand along new lines. A soldier among soldiers, in the next few years he became something more—a writer, an amateur anthropologist, an observer and recorder. To his lot it fell not to kill but to preserve.

THREE

"Glass-Eye" the Ethnologist

W HEN CHRISTIAN BARTHELMESS became an infantryman, it was in one of the old line regiments—the Thirteenth, first organized in 1798. The Thirteenth served in the War of 1812, the Mexican War, and the Civil War, in which for a time William Tecumseh Sherman was its colonel. In the period of Barthelmess' service in the Southwest, the Thirteenth's commander was Colonel Luther P. Bradley, a Civil War brigadier general of volunteers.

Barthelmess' new station, Fort Wingate, was in McKinley County, twelve miles east of Gallup and forty miles north of the old Pueblo Indian village of Zuñi, at a place called Ojo del Oso, Bear Spring, on the road to Fort Defiance. The army moved its posts in this area so often that they should have been on wheels. The first fort at Ojo del Oso was established in 1860 under the name of Fort Fauntleroy. When its namesake, Colonel Thomas T. Fauntleroy of Virginia, who had fought against the Utes in Colorado in 1855, joined the Confederacy in 1862, the post was renamed Fort Lyon. Then it was abandoned, as federal troops were sent to the Río Grande to stem a Confederate thrust northward. In 1862, at a new site sixty miles southeast, near San Rafael, Fort Wingate was established. It was a base for Kit Carson's campaign against the Navahos in 1863–64. In 1868 it was moved to the original Fauntleroy-Lyon site at Ojo del Oso. Fort Wingate was active from that time until 1910, when it was left in charge of a caretaker. It was garrisoned in 1914–15 for the purpose of guarding Mexican refugees, and in 1918 was used by the Ordnance Department for storage of high explosives. In 1925 it became a Navaho Indian school. Many of the original buildings remained until 1960, when some were razed for the erection of modern school facilities.[1]

The purpose in garrisoning Fort Wingate at Ojo del Oso in 1868 was to furnish military surveillance for the nearby Navaho reservation. And it was while Christian Barthelmess was stationed at Fort Wingate, and at his next post of duty, Fort Bayard, that he became interested in studying the Navahos, as well as photographing them. It was in this connection that he was associated with another army man, Irish born, Iowan by adoption, a man with a red beard, wearing on his uniform the shoulder straps of a major—a man who combined with his military duties a scientific study of the Navahos that was to win him recognition as "the first and foremost student" of the people of that tribe.

This man was Dr. Washington Matthews (1843–1905).[2] He had attained his M.D. degree at the University of Iowa by taking a course of lectures there following his study of medicine in his father's office. In the Civil War, Washington Matthews was an acting assistant surgeon, and in 1865 he was appointed post surgeon at Fort Union, Montana. There, and at Fort Rice, Dakota Territory, he studied the Indians of the area and compiled a 239-page *Ethnography and Philology of the Hidatsa Indians*, published in 1877 by the United States Geological and Geographical Survey (*Miscellaneous Publications No. 7*).

Matthews was post surgeon at Fort Wingate from 1880 to 1884, and spent as much time as he could take from his military duties studying the customs, ceremonies, and language of the Indians. Under auspices of the United States Bureau of Ethnology, he spent the summer of 1884 in the Navaho country, devoting himself to studies in anthropology—then a new field of research.[3] In all, he published fifty-eight monographs. He was the first enthnologist to attain an understanding of the Navahos

[1] National Park Service, *Soldier and Brave*, 203–204. Also, "History of Fort Wingate," Wingate Ordnance Reserve Depot, pamphlet, 1925.

[2] *Dictionary of American Biography*, XXII, 241. Erna Fergusson, in her *New Mexico: A Pageant of Three Peoples*, speaks of Matthews as "the first comprehending student of the Navajo ceremonies . . . who was also a musician and sensitive to beauty in any form."

[3] "A museum of anthropology was established in Hamburg in 1850; the Pea-

as people, through a study of their way of life, particularly their legends and ceremonies. And Matthews the scientist, the scholarly authority whose works are still basic to the subject, was materially aided in his research by a man with little formal education but with a sharp eye and an inquiring mind—Christian Barthelmess. In his writings, Matthews acknowledges his debt to the soldier-musician-photographer.

One of these contributions was the transcription of songs— putting into writing both the words and music which the Indians, having no written language, had previously preserved solely by word of mouth.[4]

Early in this paper, Matthews says that "for many years the most trusted account of the Navaho[5] Indians of New Mexico and Arizona was to be found in a letter written by Dr. Jonathan Letherman, of the army, and published in the Smithsonian report for 1855."[6] Dr. Letherman had lived three years at Fort Defiance, in the heart of the Navaho country. His letter of 1885 said of these Indians:

> Of their religion little or nothing is known, as indeed all inquiries tend to show that they have none. . . . The lack of tradition is a source of surprise. They have no knowledge of their origin or the history of the tribe. . . . They have frequent gatherings for dancing. . . . Their singing is but a succession of grunts, and is anything but agreeable.

body Museum of Archaeology and Ethnology at Harvard was founded in 1866; the Royal Anthropological Institute in 1873; the Bureau of American Ethnology in 1879 . . . . The first American professor was appointed in 1886. But in the nineteenth century there were not a hundred anthropologists in the whole world." (Clyde Kluckhohn, *Mirror for Man*, 12.)

[4] Volume V, *Memoirs of the American Folk-Lore Society*, published in 1897, is given over to a lengthy monograph by Matthews, entitled, "Navaho Legends." The society was organized January 4, 1888, for the collection and publication of folklore and mythology of the American continent. It published (and still does) the quarterly *Journal of American Folk-lore* and occasional *Memoirs*.

[5] In this paper, Dr. Matthews Americanized the Spanish word *Navajo* by using "h" instead of "j," which he sometimes used in other writings. The Navajo Tribal Council uses the historical spelling, presumably bestowed on the tribe by the Spaniards. The University of Oklahoma Press, like the Bureau of American Ethnology, which uses "Navaho" in *The Handbook of American Indians*, prefers the Americanized spelling. Matthews said the word meant clasp-knife or razor, or perhaps a pool or small lake. Others believe it meant large cornfields. The Navahos call themselves in their language, *Diné*, meaning "The People."

[6] Smithsonian Institution, *Tenth Annual Report*.

273. DOVE SONG.

(See par. 50.)   Music by CHRISTIAN BARTHELMESS.

Wos wos ṅai-di̓-la a a, Wos wos nai-di̓-lo o o,

Wos wos nai-di̓-la a a, Tsi-nol-ka-ꜱi nai-di̓-la a a,

Ke-ʌ-tsi-tsi nai-di̓-la a a, Wos wos nai-di̓-lo o o.

TEXTS AND INTERLINEAR TRANSLATIONS.

274. ASSEVERATION OF TORLINO (IN PART).

Naestsán   bayántsĭn.
Earth (Woman Horizontal), for it I am ashamed.

Yádĭlyĭl   bayántsĭn.
Sky (dark above), for it I am ashamed.

Hayolkáł   bayántsĭn,
Dawn,   for it I am ashamed.

Naẖotsói   bayántsĭn.
Evening (Land of Horizontal   for it I am ashamed.
      Yellow),

Naẖodoʈlĭ́ꜱi   bayántsĭn.
Blue sky (Land or Place of   for it I am ashamed.
     Horizontal Blue),

Tsałyél   bayántsĭn.
Darkness,   for it I am ashamed.

Tsóhanoai   bayántsĭn.
Sun,   for it I am ashamed.

Si sĭzíni beyaꜱʈĭ'yi   bayántsĭn.
In me it stands, with me it talks, for it I am ashamed.

The "Dove Song," words in Navaho, music transcribed by Christian Barthelmess in *Memoirs of the American Folk-Lore Society*, V (1897), 258.

Dr. Matthews, coming to the Navahos in 1880, refused to accept this concept, and began to explore the matter for himself. He had not been long in New Mexico, he writes, before he learned that the dances to which Dr. Letherman referred were religious ceremonials, and that they "might vie in allegory, symbolism, and intricacy of ritual with the ceremonies of any people, ancient or modern." Matthews found, "ere long, that these heathens, pronounced godless and legendless," in fact possessed myths and traditions "so numerous that one can never hope to collect them all, a pantheon as well stocked with gods and heroes as that of the ancient Greeks." And the "appalling succession of grunts" convinced Matthews that besides improvised songs, "in which the Navahos are adept, they have knowledge of thousands of significant songs—or poems, as they might be called—which have been composed with care and handed down, for centuries perhaps, from teacher to pupil, from father to son, a precious heritage."[7]

Twenty-eight songs which Dr. Matthews recorded on phonograph records and then had transcribed by musicians are printed in his 1897 monograph, "Navaho Legends," as written in musical notation. Twenty-seven of the songs were transcribed by Professor John Comfort Fillmore, of Milwaukee, Wisconsin, and Claremont, California.[8] The twenty-eighth song was transcribed by Christian Barthelmess and is credited to him in Matthews' article in *Memoirs of the American Folk-Lore Society* (page 258). It is the following "Dove Song."

> *Wos Wos picks them* [*seeds*] *up,*
> *Wos Wos picks them up,*
> *Glossy Locks picks them up,*
> *Red Moccasin picks them up,*
> *Wos Wos picks them up.*

[7] "Navaho Legends," *Memoirs*, Vol. V, paragraphs 36–40. In *Masked Gods*, Frank Waters says that "as translations multiply, we are beginning to recognize the lyrics of the Navajo songs as pure poetry. Great poetry. Its rhythm sings even in the printed word. It abounds with metaphors and similes so subtle as to be almost incomprehensible to those who do not know the country and the intense feeling it evokes" (p. 251).

[8] Fillmore (1843–98) founded the Milwaukee Music School in 1884, and in 1895 became director of the Pomona College Music School at Claremont, Cali-

Dr. Matthews explains this as one of a large number of songs used in the Navaho ceremonial gambling game called *kesitce* (from *ke*, meaning moccasins, and *sitce*, side by side); the players guess in which of several moccasins laid parallel to each other are hidden certain objects such as seeds, stones, or sticks. It is a game common, with variations, to many tribes. Many *kesitce* songs, Dr. Matthews comments, allude to recondite matters of symbolism, or mythological incidents, which could be made understandable to non-Navahos only with difficulty; but, he adds, "some of the metaphors and similes are not so hard to understand," and he cites the "Dove Song" as an example:

"Here Wos Wos [pronounced Wōsh Wōsh] is an onomatope[9] for dove, equivalent to our 'coo-coo'; but it is used as a noun. Glossy Locks and Red Moccasin are figurative expressions for the dove, of obvious significance. Metaphor and synecdoche[10] are here combined." Dr. Matthews further comments on this and the other songs as throwing light on the problem of the form spontaneously assumed by natural folksongs. These "carry us back toward the beginnings of music making." The sounds themselves do resemble howling more than singing, "yet they are unmistakably musical in two particulars: Strongly marked rhythm and harmonic relations to the successive tones."

Earlier in his writings about the Navahos,[11] Dr. Matthews speaks of two dove songs, referring to the one previously discussed as No. 2. The No. 1 song is, in English translation:

> The dove flies, the dove flies,
> The dove flies, the dove flies,
> Toward the white alkali flat the dove flies.

Other animals celebrated in similar songs are the little owl,

---

fornia. He not only was influential in placing music in college curricula but also became an authority on Indian music.

[9] An onomatope is a word formed by onomatopoeia, which is the use of words whose sounds seem to resemble sounds they describe.

[10] Synecdoche signifies a part of something representative of the whole.

[11] "Navajo Gambling Songs," in *The American Anthropologist*, Vol. II, No. 1 (January, 1889), 1.

the bear, magpie, chicken hawk, gopher, badger, snake, ground squirrel, and wildcat. The "Chicken Hawk" song:

> *The old owl hates me.*
> *When alone I always bring home abundance*
> *of rabbits, that is why he hates me.*

The "Bear Song":

> *With these four, these four, these four, these four,*
> *These four things to walk with, whence comes he?*
> *With these four, these four, these four, these four,*
> *These four shaggy things to walk with, whence comes he?*

One can only imagine what satisfaction the young soldier from Bavaria derived from contributing to the anthropological information that another soldier, the eminent Dr. Matthews, was compiling about the Navahos. If Christian Barthelmess ever knew that his name appeared in this connection in a learned dissertation, he did not reveal it to his family. Even his son Casey was unaware of the extent of his association with Dr. Matthews until research for this book disclosed not only the foregoing, but also further contributions that Christian Barthelmess had made to early information about the Navahos.

Two articles were written in German by Barthelmess and printed in 1883 and 1884 in a German newspaper, *Der Westen*, then published in Chicago. Dr. Matthews had preserved tear sheets of the articles, which were found among voluminous papers comprising the Matthews Collection in the Museum of Navajo Ceremonial Art, Santa Fe, New Mexico.[12] (There also is a tear sheet of an article which Matthews had written in English and Barthelmess had translated into German, published October 14, 1883, in *Der Westen* under the title *"Ein Theil der Navajoe Mythologie"*—"A Bit of Navaho Mythology.") The first

[12] The Washington Matthews collection is in the research department of the museum. After Matthews' death, in 1905, his papers were deposited in the Anthropology Department of the University of California. More than fifty years later, they were transferred to the Santa Fe museum. The collection includes manuscripts, notebooks, proof sheets, photographs, drawings, and miscellaneous papers. A 100-page typed catalog of the collection was prepared by Elsbeth E. Freudenthal in 1951.

of the two articles that Barthelmess wrote appeared in *Der Westen* on April 8, 1883. It describes a Navaho ceremony held for the purpose of curing a sick man.

His second article, January 17, 1884, describes a ceremony to assure the continued good health of a person who has been cured—in this instance, a girl. Concerning this second article, Matthews has written as follows:[13]

> In the winter of 1883–4 while at Fort Wingate, New Mexico, I made arrangements to attend a ceremony of the night chant at a point some 14 miles from the post. When the time came for me to depart, I was detained by professional duties. A member of the Regimental Band of the 13th Infantry, Sergeant Christian Barthelmess, who took a deep and intelligent interest in ethnographic studies, expressed a desire to go. I obtained for him a short leave, gave him a mount, and arranged with the Indians for a kindly reception for him. He arrived at the medicine-lodge on the ninth day of the ceremony, saw the outdoor rites of the afternoon and the outdoor dance at night. He observed well, and wrote an excellent account of what he saw, which was published in a German paper of Chicago, *Der Westen*, in January, 1884.

Thus Barthelmess served as a stand-in for Matthews, and was undoubtedly one of the earliest non-Indians to attend a Navaho "sing," or ceremony, for the purpose of preserving it as a part of the records of a people whose old way of life was even then fast fading. Barthelmess' resultant articles comprise the next two chapters of this book.

[13] *Memoirs of the American Museum of Natural History*, Vol. VI (May, 1902), 310–11.

FOUR

Old Bear Face and a Fire Dance

THE NAVAHOS, numerically the largest of the North American Indian tribes, were little known to the people of the United States when Musician Barthelmess of the Thirteenth Infantry photographed them and wrote about them in 1883 and 1884. The early Spanish explorers had left some written records of their contacts with the Navahos in the sixteenth and seventeenth centuries, and missionaries had been among them in the eighteenth century, but had made little impress. In 1849, when the United States took possession of New Mexico, the Navahos were engaged in a running war with the Pueblos and the few white settlers. They were a nomadic and warlike people, living in a land of great deserts and little water, subsisting on meager crops of corn, beans, squash, and melons, and pasturing sheep and goats on what little forage could be found.

The first American military expedition into Navaho-land was led by Colonel Alexander W. Doniphan, of Kearney's Army of the West, which conquered New Mexico in 1846. On behalf of the United States, Doniphan made a transitory treaty with the Navahos in November of that year. In 1849, another military force, under Colonel John M. Washington, penetrated the Navaho country as far as the Canyon de Chelly, and another treaty was made, but the peace was not lasting. In 1863, Colonel Kit Carson, with an army of New Mexico volunteers, harassed the Navahos through the summer and winter and threatened them with starvation by killing off most of their sheep. They took refuge in the Canyon de Chelly, where, in January of 1864, Carson and his men captured some 7,000 of them and took them on their tragic "Long Walk" to Bosque Redondo (Round Grove) on the Pecos River in eastern New Mexico, where they were kept until 1868. Then they were allowed to return to their old home in the Fort Defiance and Canyon de Chelly country, where a reservation of some 5,200 square miles—later greatly increased—was assigned to them. The 1890 census showed that there were 17,204 Navahos.[1] By 1965 they numbered about 90,000, and were adjusting to the modern world at a steadily accelerating rate.

When young Barthelmess knew the Navahos, in the early 1880's, they were not much removed from the primitive, a fact that lends importance to his descriptions of their ways and to photographs he made then. Extracted from the dust it gathered for eighty years in the files of *Der Westen*, and translated into English,[2] here follows his account of what he called a *Medizin-Tanz*, or medicine dance—in this case, a nine-day rite for healing of the sick:

"I had long had the intention of visiting the Navahos on their reservation in order to study—and to photograph—their usages, customs and dances. Since the officers of Fort Wingate had given me the opportunity to accompany them to a Medicine Dance, I assembled my gear [*packte ich meine sieben Sachen zusammen*, or packed together my seven things] and prepared to join the party. When I reached Fort Wingate, I found that the group had left about an hour earlier and, mounted on an old nag, I tried to overtake them. About four miles from the Fort I met an old Indian and his squaw, who told me, in a wonderful mixture of English, Spanish, and Navaho, that the company was about four miles ahead. Spurring my jaded steed to greater speed, I entered a valley just in time to see my friends disappear out the other end. I wasn't more than ten miles from Fort Wingate and my horse already showed signs of weariness. In spite of all my efforts, I could not overtake my friends. Since their company was composed of seven mounted officers, five

[1] Department of the Interior, *Report on Indians Taxed and Indians Not Taxed in the United States (except Alaska) at the Eleventh Census: 1890.*

[2] By Margaret W. (Mrs. William S.) Jackson, of Denver, Colorado, who also translated the article comprising Chapter Five.

soldiers, and two pack animals, it had been easy for me to follow their trail. But when I had followed this obvious trail through the valley and found other tracks which joined in with those I had been following, things became more difficult, especially when other shod horses took up the trail.

"I followed this trail until about four o'clock in the afternoon when my horse turned off to the left. Since most of the tracks took this direction, I accepted the animal's judgment and rode along for about three miles when all signs of tracks were lost in loose gravel. With great difficulty I picked up the trail farther on. My horse lost a shoe and went lame and refused to go on. I took my camera, tripod, and saddlebag over my shoulder and trudged ahead on foot. It was already getting dark when I came upon a so-called 'hogan' (Indian hut) where I found an old deaf squaw and a seven-year-old girl. It was impossible to make myself understood because the old woman couldn't hear and the little girl didn't understand Spanish. All I could make out was that there was a *camino grande* [main road] the other side of the valley and four miles farther on lived a bearded American.

"I continued on my way and found the main road, but I didn't know which way to go. To the north was a great plain, to the south were the mountains. Since it did not seem likely that a pioneer settled in this district would engage in anything but cattle raising, I decided that the bearded American lived in the mountains where wood and water were plentiful. Like a silly Swabian[3] I fumbled ahead, leading my horse by the reins until the beast lay down and, in spite of all my begging and pleading and the lash of a whip, refused to move. I did the only thing I could do—unsaddled, made a fire, and prepared to spend the night in the open. Under ordinary circumstances this would have been neither new nor unpleasant to me, but this time it was most uncomfortable. The temperature was less than warm; a light rain had soaked me thoroughly; except for a small saddle blanket I had nothing to pull on and was also without weapons.

[3] Swabia was a medieval German duchy, comprising Baden, Würtenberg, and part of Bavaria and Switzerland, named for the ancient Suevi.

Because this affair, which I had thought to attend, was a nice occasion, and I was to return shortly, I had left blankets and weapons behind and brought with me only my hunting knife.

"Since there wasn't much wood about, I made a small fire of brush wood and stretched out on my little blanket, lighting the pipe which was my only consolation. Suddenly it seemed to me that I saw in the distance a light which vanished as quickly as it appeared. Finally I saw it again and realized that there was a fire in the distance. I saddled up—even my tired nag seemed to have noticed something—and set out briskly.

"After about an hour I was greeted by barking dogs and stood before an Indian hut. Fortunately one of the squaws understood Spanish and even some English. After I had explained my situation and asked for a night's lodging, I was admitted and lay down by the fire. For fifty cents I bought some corn and another fifty cents got water for my horse. The household consisted of two women and a young and very beautiful girl about fourteen years of age. From the father of the family I discovered that he had seen my friends and knew where they were camped. I promised him three dollars if he would seek them out and deliver a message to them. He went out to find a horse, but had no luck and returned to wait for daylight.

"Meantime I had made myself comfortable, and from the two women I tried to learn a little Navaho. The pronunciation is very hard for a German and my efforts gave rise to much merriment. After I had written about a dozen words in my notebook, I fell asleep.

"I woke the Indian early so that he could carry out his mission. I prepared some coffee, without which I never travel, and gave him some and sent him on his way. I then set out to look for my horse, and found him about a mile from the hut.

"The sun had just come up and shone in all its glory. The Indian hut was on a little hill and was surrounded by herds of sheep. The women were making preparations to go to the dance. I sat down on a stone and looked at this beautiful scene. It was Sunday morning; quite spontaneously I sang some lines from Abt's 'On Sunday':

The shepherds are resting among the herds
And the lambs are asleep in the meadow.[4]

"In order to preserve this picture, I got my camera and photographed it. About ten o'clock my redskin appeared with a cavalryman and a fresh horse. The cavalryman told me that their camp where the dance was to take place was about twelve miles away. They had become worried about me and had sent a message back to Wingate to find out where I was. After a second breakfast I saddled my fresh horse and gave the weary nag to the Indian to ride to the dance. We set out at a gallop. It took the Indian, the cavalryman, and me an hour and a quarter to cover the twelve miles. We arrived just in time for lunch and I did not delay taking a picture of the group immediately we got there.

"The Indian Agent Riordan[5] from Fort Defiance, Arizona, with an interpreter, had arrived. He was to hold a conference that same day with the tribal chiefs. The Indians had gathered in great numbers and were camped about in colorful groups. Some played cards, some lay in the sun and smoked cigarettes, others played a game for which I could find no name, but which I shall attempt to describe. Two teams played alternately, each team consisting of two men. Each player had a long staff, something like a fishpole. A wooden ring was rolled along an even track and the staffs were thrown parallel to the path the rolling ring took. Whoever came the nearest the ring won. I could not discover how the different throws were scored. I took a picture of the game and spectators.

"Next I paid a visit to the gentler sex, who were also absorbed in a game. By a circle about three feet in diameter made of small stones sat the two players. In the middle of this circle was a stone about a foot square, toward which each of the players

---

4 Franz Abt (1819–85) was a German composer whose songs were popular at the middle of the nineteenth century.

5 The Navaho superintendent, appointed by President Chester A. Arthur. "Hard-headed politician though he was, Denis M. Riordan showed what could be done with the Navajos by intimate, friendly relationship. They talk yet about his trips among them, when the white man in his fur cap sat down and talked things over 'like a relative.' . . . one of the few early agents who really saw the Indians and thought about them . . . ." (Ruth M. Underhill, *The Navajos*, 172.)

threw three pieces of wood which were held pressed together in the right hand. The score was reckoned on the fall of the pieces of wood as they bounced off the center stone either inside or outside the circle; also considered was the distance between the pieces of wood and the stones which formed the circle. To keep the pieces of wood from flying too far and too high, there was a sort of canopy over the game space.

"I had a great deal of trouble getting a picture of this group because the squaws were not inclined to sit still and as a result I got an incomplete picture.

"The Indians had already gathered for their council meeting when I joined them to listen. I had already heard that Riordan, the agent, was going to give the Indians a stern lecture about stealing horses; he was determined to have it out with them. First Manuelito,[6] the peace chief, gave a long talk which was very boring to me because I didn't understand a word he said. Then various less important chiefs spoke and finally it was Riordan's turn. First he told the Indians that in the different councils he had had with their chiefs he had promised to persuade the Great Father in Washington that the reservation should be enlarged; this he had done. The Indians, for their part, had promised to abstain from stealing, to give up drinking brandy [*das Branntweinsaufen aufzugeben*] and to lead orderly and honorable lives. Many had not kept their promise! Letter after letter had come in with complaints of their behavior; he himself had followed a horse thief for weeks, had retrieved the stolen property but the thief had escaped. As long as the Indians wouldn't forego their vices, and become better men, he could do nothing more for them.

"A Mexican appeared and complained that he had lost 150 sheep during the last snowstorm. He well knew that the large

[6] Barthelmess spells the name Manulito, but obviously was speaking of Manuelito, a famous chief, whom Ruth M. Underhill in *The Navajos* speaks of (p. 134) as "the handsome warrior of the powerful voice," who was "all Navajo and all fighter." He once led an attack on Fort Defiance, and his band was among the last to come in at Fort Sumner when the Navahos capitulated to Kit Carson. In 1868 he was one of the signers of the treaty under which the Navahos returned to Fort Defiance. The town of Manuelito, just west of Gallup, preserves his name.

Chris Barthelmess doffed his army uniform and wore a borrowed scout outfit when this picture was taken in 1886 in Mrs. Albright's Art Parlors, Albuquerque, N. M., when he was a musician in the Thirteenth Infantry at Fort Bayard, N. M. He took the picture of Mrs. Barthelmess in his Fort Keogh studio in the early 1890's.

Here Casey Barthelmess is shown on his first outing, a picnic near Fort Keogh. He is in his mother's arms, center of the group, with Leo and Florence at her feet. The soldier on the left has picked up Christian Barthelmess' violin, which he had laid down to pick up his camera.

Fort Keogh, about 1896: Quartermaster stables, teamster quarters, mess, blacksmith shop, and (with open doors) a building where loaded water wagons served as fire protection. Children are Casey, Florence, Adelaide, and Leo Barthelmess. Center, an army escort wagon, horse watering trough, and water wagon.

The Thirteenth Infantry band at the Winslow, Ariz., station of the Atchison, Topeka & Santa Fe Railway, 1882 or 1883, on an excursion from Fort Wingate, N. M. Band-member Barthelmess is in the picture. (Photograph not taken by Barthelmess.)

The Second Infantry band, to which Barthelmess belonged,
leading a column of Fort Keogh troops on a practice march
along Tongue River in 1896, pauses for the Barthelmess camera.
On the right stands a bicycle soldier, his rifle slung on the frame
of his wheel.

A German singing society of the Twenty-second Infantry, conducted by Musician Barthelmess.

Twenty-second Infantry band in full dress, in front of the band quarters at Keogh, with Christian Barthelmess seated left. (Photograph not taken by Barthelmess.)

Fort Wingate, N. M., Barthelmess' station with the Thirteenth Infantry, about 1881. Here he began his association with anthropologist Washington Matthews, an army assistant surgeon.

Fort Bayard, N. M., where Barthelmess was discharged in 1886 at the end of his second enlistment, and where he re-enlisted in the Twenty-second Infantry.

An outpost at Emory Springs, Perilla Mountains, Cochise County, Ariz.; Sixth Cavalry Apache scouts.

"Some of our White Mountain Apache scouts." The man second from left wears an ancient Apache war cap.

Fort Lewis, Colo., where Barthelmess served, 1887–88, in the Twenty-second Infantry. Here he began his acquaintance with the ill-fated Lt. Casey, and with Col. Peter Tyler Swaine, commander of the Twenty-second and later post commander at Fort Keogh.

"Some Ute police of White River Agency." Barthelmess does not say where he encountered these Utes. The White River Ute Agency was in northwestern Colo. (Río Blanco County), and was the scene of the Meeker massacre of 1879.

Col. Peter T. Swaine, commanding Twenty-second Infantry, Fort Lewis, Colo., 1887, relaxes (left) on a fishing trip on the Pine River. Center, Mrs. Swaine; right, Capt. William Conway; left, Mrs. Conway; officer in rear unidentified. The youth is the Swaines' son William.

Lt. Kell, Capt. C. W. Miner, and Lt. Jones at an unnamed Colorado mountain lake near Fort Lewis.

Prehistoric dwellings in Canyon de Chelly, near Fort Defiance, 1887. The man at left center is dwarfed by the towering cliff, with houses at two elevations.

majority had died in the snowstorm, but about 50 of them were to be found in an Indian's herd with their brand marks changed.

"It was explained that this Indian belonged to no definite tribe and merely hung around the Navahos. The agent told the Mexican that if he were willing to be the guide, he (the agent) would, if necessary, provide soldiers to help him regain his sheep. The Mexican agreed to this and, after further warnings from the agent, the gathering broke up.

"Part of the Indians remained behind, to speak of other things. The result of this conversation was that on the next morning the chiefs appeared and guaranteed that the sheep would be returned, if only the military would not be called out and the Great Father would not think badly of them.

"The evening drew near and preparations for the dance began. It was performed to restore a patient to health.[7] The ceremony had already lasted nine days and was to be concluded with the dance that evening. The ceremonial lodge was about twenty feet in diameter, with a pointed roof. The outside walls were sod; there were a door and a chimney. A curtain hung over the door, and at the threshold bundles of eagle feathers and stalks of blooming maize were stuck in the earth. The area where the dance was to take place was fenced in with evergreen boughs and was about sixty yards across. In the middle was a huge pile of wood, which was to be the ceremonial fire. Within the enclosure, near the evergreen fence, were many small piles of wood which were the campfires for the guests. The entrance was toward the east, and all traffic must go from left to right. By the time darkness fell, our whole company was gathered within this circle, and all obeyed the rules with care.

[7] Frank Waters, *Masked Gods*, 255, says: "The primary function if not the sole purpose of Navaho sings is to cure illness of the body and mind. . . . The ceremonial thus considered is a vast and complex thaumaturgical [miraculous] rite which has its parallels in modern Western psychotherapy, Christian Science, and Buddhist yoga." Waters says (p. 256) that even among modern-day Navahos, the power of these ceremonies is considered so great that no person is thought to be strong enough to conduct one of them unless one has been held for him as the patient. Waters quotes "the pioneer" Washington Matthews as saying that mistakes made in a Night Chant caused crippling and paralysis, and that, "peculiarly enough, he himself [Matthews] suffered a paralytic stroke while learning it."

"About a quarter before nine o'clock the singers appeared—twenty-five or thirty of them—and let their melody, or better, their howling, ring forth. At nine o'clock the huge pile of wood was ignited, and the arrival of the dancers was announced by a shrill blast on a wooden whistle. The dance followed various patterns, rather like a quadrille. First the medicine man appeared, one of the ugliest figures I have ever seen. Most of his nose had been destroyed by cancer, or some such disease, and as a result his voice had a horrible twang such as I had never before heard.[8] Following him came sixteen young Indians, all of them in Adam's costume except for a small apron hung about the hips; each held a two-foot-long staff on which were tied small bits of wool. The medicine man shook an instrument rather like a child's rattle.

"The dance followed this order:[9]

"First there were three jumps forward, then a half turn to the right with bent knees, then all remained motionless, then the man at the rear stepped with his right leg through the legs of the man in front and turned also. This was repeated three times circling about the fire. Then the dancers returned to the medicine lodge which was about one hundred yards away. After a quarter of an hour the whistle shrilled again and the second part of the dance began. This time the dancers jumping forward and backward circled the fire. This happened four times. When they had finished with the round dance, they danced on the east side, zigzagging toward the fire and back, then they jumped one

[8] This was a Navaho named Old Bear Face. He was a Mountain Chant singer, and derived his name from the fact that his face was clawed by a bear cub he had trained to appear in the ninth night of the Mountain Chant. In his second article in *Der Westen*, in 1884 (see Chapter Five), Barthelmess corrects his statement that the disfigurement was due to disease. Old Bear Face's ceremonial objects are housed in the American Museum of Natural History, New York. (Informant, Mrs. Evelyn Dahl, Museum of Navajo Ceremonial Art, Santa Fe, New Mexico.)

[9] "This is a description of the Fire Dance, which takes place on the ninth night of the Mountain Chant. The staffs mentioned are probably the firebrands, made of bundles of bark. Four are used by each of the dancers. They are lighted at the fire, used to flagellate the dancers, and then tossed in each of the four directions. The Museum of Navajo Ceremonial Art has on film a motion picture of the Fire Dance and other rites of a healing ceremony, as performed in the 1920's." (Mrs. Evelyn Dahl.)

after the other right up to the fire and burnt the wool balls on the tips of the staffs. That was not a bit easy. We were about thirty yards from the fire and found the heat unendurable and had to draw back beyond the fence. Just think of the heat the Indians had to withstand until the balls of wool were burnt from the ends of their staffs!

"Next the dancers appeared again with an Indian boy hardly five years old; he was (un)dressed like the others and held in each hand a sort of cross decorated with eagle feathers. The dancers grouped themselves again in a half-circle, and the boy danced alone in time with the singing, first slowly and then faster and faster. It was astonishing with what precision he kept time. In the next figure, two dancers appeared, their heads and arms decorated with feathered arrows and each carrying an arrow in his right hand. The patient was raised up on a buffalo robe, and the performers danced at his feet.

"First each drew an arrow through his mouth, then turned to the north and, with raised arm, let out a Navaho war-whoop. Then they bowed their heads as far as they could and slowly put the arrows back in the quiver, stamping and moving forward in short steps. The arrows were drawn out again, and the war-whoop was given again. The sick person sat up, and the dancers touched his limbs with the arrows. Now the little boy's dance was repeated three times.

"In the next figure the dancers appeared accompanied by a sacred clown [German *Bajazzo*, or buffoon] in a fool's cap. After the clown had told several jokes, which were greeted with hearty laughter, the dancers formed a close circle and began to sing. The fool tried to break into the circle but was not successful; when the dancers separated, one could see a hundred-year Agave,[10] which grows by the thousands in Arizona and New Mexico. Then the dancers closed ranks, and when they separated a second time, the plant was covered with blossoms; a third opening of the dancers' ranks showed fruit on the plant.

---

[10] A genus of amaryllidaceous plants of tropical America and southwestern United States. Several species possess detergent properties and are known as amoles, or soap plants, and in Mexico as the maguey. The fleshy-leafed century plant, or American aloe, presumably is intended here.

"In the next figure various dancers came out like those already described, decorated with arrows; they went through the same routines as before except that when they had finished with the sick man, they jumped around the fire four times and then withdrew.

"Since I had had very little sleep the night before and had been short on rest the week before, as a result of a trip to Zuñi where I had photographed Zuñi dances and another trip to Albuquerque where I had played for a dance (I am a musician with the Thirteenth Infantry Regiment), I was overcome with weariness and lay back and fell asleep.

"It was three o'clock in the morning and the dance ended about four o'clock and most of the guests departed.

"At sunrise I took a picture of the dance with the fire still burning. The sick man sent a message asking if I would 'look at him through the glass,' since he would like to send a picture to his brother in Carlisle, Pennsylvania.[11] This seemed to me surprising, since the Navaho hates to be photographed and frequently has to be well paid before he will pose. I took the picture with him and Manuelito on horseback with the little boy dancer in the middle; the background was composed of the medicine lodge surrounded by soldiers and Indians.

"After I had bought various beautiful examples of Navaho blankets and breakfast was taken care of, we saddled up and set out for home. My horse gave out again, and only with great difficulty and after I had walked great stretches did we arrive about five o'clock in the evening at Fort Wingate. My only weapon, my hunting knife, had somehow been taken from me, somewhere along the way."

[11] Ruth M. Underhill, *The Navajos*, 307, says six Navahos were enrolled in 1885 at the Carlisle Indian School. This school had been opened in 1879 in abandoned army quarters at Carlisle Barracks, Pennsylvania, near Harrisburg. Founder and superintendent at the school for twenty-five years was Captain (later Brigadier General) Richard Henry Pratt of New York, who had served in the Civil War and with the Tenth Cavalry on the Southern Plains. The government's first off-reservation boarding school for Indians, Carlisle closed in 1918. Pratt died in 1924. See Elaine Goodale Eastman, *Pratt: The Red Man's Moses*, and Robert M. Utley, *Battlefield and Classroom*.

FIVE

A Noho-tschin-tchal for Mariana

T O HIS ARTICLE about Old Bear Face and the fire dance, printed April 8, 1883, in *Der Westen*, Christian Barthelmess added a note inviting readers interested in buying Navaho pictures to write to Barthelmess & Schofield, Fort Wingate, New Mexico. This was his "business address" during a period when he was stationed at that post and was doing some of his camera work in collaboration with another photographer. Barthelmess also wrote, at the end of his article, "This is my first attempt; should it find pleasure in the eyes of your readers I will follow it with others." And so, on January 17, 1884, his second description of a Navaho ritual reached print. A translation follows:[1]

"Probably readers of *Der Westen* will remember my article of last year which described a Navaho medicine dance. Since then I have learned that among the Navahos not only medicine dances but other ceremonials are used to cure the sick, and that there are also ceremonies performed to keep the recuperated patient in good health. Apparently the Navahos believe an ounce of prevention is worth a pound of cure.

---

[1] Mrs. Evelyn Dahl, Museum of Navajo Ceremonial Art, Santa Fe, New Mexico, who read the manuscript of this chapter and Chapter Four, comments as follows: "This is a description of the Flintway ceremony, or Knife Chant, classified as a Lifeway ritual of the Navajos. Flintway is thought to be obsolete now, but one can never be sure. In any case, Barthelmess has accurately recorded the ritual items, procedures, and body painting." Mrs. Dahl, in verifying or correcting Navaho words in the Barthelmess text, has for consistency in spelling followed the Franciscan Fathers' *A Vocabulary of the Navajo Language*. She remarks: "There are as many ways of putting down Navaho sounds as there are writers of them. Barthelmess' *noho-tschin-tchal*, for instance, has also been written *jin-no-ho-hateral*. Ceremonial names used by Barthelmess are in archaic language at best. Some, like 'Glass Eye' and 'petticoat,' are made up colloquially."

"The healing ceremonies, for the most part dances, are called *no-tschin-tchal*; those ceremonies which preserve the health are known as *da-cho* or *noho-tschin-tchal*. In the former there is dancing and singing, in the latter only singing. The former ceremonies last for nine days and close with a big dance; in the latter case the ceremonies are concluded in two nights.

"A short time ago I had the opportunity of seeing a *noho-tschin-tchal*. The ceremonies of the first night were already in full swing when, attracted by the sound of singing, I tried to enter the hogan. In a room about eighteen feet in diameter, some fifty Indians were crowded, so that there wasn't a single spot where I could have settled down. On the second evening, I got to the place early, and my full tobacco pouch and cigarette papers got me a good place. At that time there were present about twenty Indians, for the most part elderly, who were listening to a story, to the telling of which the oldest man present was giving his best. I understood that the yarn concerned both Mexicans and Americans, but that there was no agreement about a count of years. Suddenly the narrator pointed his finger at me and demanded: 'How long has it been since the Americans came into this country?' I replied, 'More than thirty-seven years.' This seemed to agree with his reckoning. Certain other fragments that I gathered from the talk convinced me that the narrator had accompanied the first expedition into Navaho territory and had attended a council meeting on this occasion. (Without doubt this expedition was the one which Colonel Doniphan, under command of General Kearny, undertook against the Navahos. He left Santa Fe on the twenty-sixth of October, 1846. At Albuquerque, New Mexico, he divided his troops in two parts. It was Gilpin[2] who held council with the Navahos under Chief Zarcillo Largo [Long Earrings] at Ojo del Oso.)

"The cigarettes had been smoked and the story concluded when the owner of the hogan appeared with a camp kettle of coffee and several plates of Navaho bread. This bread is a cross between the Mexican *tortilla* and the American flapjack. Every-

[2] William Gilpin, first territorial governor of Colorado (1861–62), was a major in Doniphan's Missouri Volunteers in 1846.

one helped himself and even I, for better or for worse, had to take part in the meal. I was not to be envied, for I had only too often watched the preparation of this bread and had not found cleanliness among the virtues of the cooks.

"The meal was over and preparations were started for the *noho-tschin-tchal*. The Indians apparently had not expected that my visit was for the whole evening and had welcomed me with politeness when I came in. But when they saw that I made no motion to leave, they began to object to my presence. I could not decide whether some of them did this so I would pay them something, or whether they really did not want strangers admitted. But I decided to remain and since I was in the neighborhood of the Post, there was nothing to fear. There was a long argument until finally some of my Navaho friends joined in and spoke in my favor. In the end I was allowed to remain, but had to promise that I would not write anything down. Naturally I promised and pocketed my notebook, which I had been holding in my hand.

"People now divided themselves into two groups, one on each side. All the Indians who had been outside came crowding into the hut, which soon was crammed full. The chief medicine man of the tribe also appeared at this time—the same horrible person whom I described in my article last year [Old Bear Face]. I can now correct certain elements of my former description, because it was not illness that had disfigured him so terribly, but a bear which had clawed away the man's forehead, nose, and upper lip. He was accompanied by a second medicine man whom I had never seen before. The first one was the one who cured the sick; his companion maintained the health of the recovered patient. In the future we will refer to them as Number 1 and Number 2. They were followed by a ten-year-old girl, Mariana, the granddaughter of the war chief; she had just recovered from an illness and the *noho-tschin-tchal* was being performed for her benefit. Number 1 took a position opposite the door in the middle of the cleared place between the two groups of onlookers. Number 2 sat at his right and the girl at his left. A buffalo robe was spread out before the three, and on this a new white cloth, and on this a freshly tanned deerskin. The magic objects which were to be used this evening would be spread out on the deerskin.

"First came the shell of a turtle filled with medicine water, and several deerskin bags which contained the medicine to be used. There was also a little wooden staff, one end of which was decorated with feathers, which would be used to administer the medicine; there were two crane's heads and several coral necklaces, the latter to be given to the girl and to be worn the rest of her life.

"The monotonous singsong began. The singing was accompanied by an instrument called in Navaho *a-kesh-gan-aghal* [hoof rattle], which was made of fawn's hooves strung on leather thongs and tied into a bundle. When shaken, this instrument produces a clear, almost metallic sound. The overture lasted about half an hour, and when it was over and they were about to begin again, the girl was relieved of all her adornments—coral necklaces, silver bracelets, and a silver belt.

"During the next song the girl's skirt and moccasins were removed and, clad only in her petticoat (in Navaho, *kla-kalch*), she was led by Number 2 to a place before the magic objects. There was a pause, of how many bars I do not know, since there was no musical score. When things began again, Number 2 painted the soles of the girl's feet, the brachial joints and muscles of her arms, her breast, and forehead with paint made of red ocher (to represent blood) and sheep tallow. During the next song he painted her whole upper body, including face and neck, with the same color. The rest of her body, which was covered by her petticoat, was painted by her grandmother.

"As soon as these two had finished the painting, what was left of the coloring matter was passed about among the audience, who smeared their breasts, legs, and faces with it. I was given some and was supposed to paint my face with it, but I preferred to put it in my pocket. Each time a ceremony was finished, there was a little pause during which the singers caught their breath and got a drink of water. It was astonishing to me that none of them became hoarse, and in certain cases, I would have been rather pleased if they had because some of them sang off key and in high treble. Each time I heard them, I was almost beside myself.

"During the next song, medicine man Number 2, using black medicine (*aze-qa-jini*) from the gromwell plant,[3] painted a black stripe across the girl's chin, and others who were given some of the black paint [charcoal] did the same.

"Now the girl was allowed to sit down, but the singing went on. Up until this time the two groups of singers seemed to be singing together, but not so now. It seemed to me a kind of song contest, for the audience called words of encouragement first to this group and then to the other. When this episode was finished, the girl returned to her original place, and Number 2 fastened in the hair over her forehead the bundle of feathers (*eltlo*, head plume) which has been mentioned. The general singing stopped suddenly and the two medicine men sang a long, melancholy-sounding song. During this, Number 2 held his right hand over the girl's head as if blessing her. When this ceremony was ended, the girl again took up her place beside Number 1, where she remained the rest of the evening.

"Now the magic objects were brought out. The two cranes' heads were fastened together by the bills and the singers sang over them a long time. When this was over, the turtle shell, filled with liquid, was given to the girl, and in three swallows she drained it and then licked out the inside.

"The medicine man then dried the shell carefully and thoroughly with a piece of deerskin. Now the real medicine, which was in the deerskin bag, was served.

"Four times the girl was given three successive doses with the feathered staff (*delda*, crane bill). With this ceremony the first and most important part of the *noho-tschin-tchal* came to an end.

"The singing stopped, and once more the camp kettle and the griddlecakes were brought out. No one was happier than I. For nearly six hours I had hardly been able to move. The only movement I could manage was to change from a kneeling to a squatting position. My legs hurt, and it was at first impossible

[3] A boraginaceous plant of the genus *Lithospermum*; also called gray millet.

for me to stand up. When I finally managed to get up, I slipped outside and walked up and down until I felt better. Afraid of missing some of the ceremony, I went back to my place inside as soon as I could and once more, with some dread, took some of the food. My stomach began to growl because I hadn't had much to eat all day and at the earlier meal I had taken very little. The coffee tasted especially good to me, and I must say it was far better than the usual army coffee.

"Everyone was very gay during the refreshment period. Good and bad jokes were made. I suffered especially from the latter. Because I am near-sighted, I have to wear spectacles. The Navahos call me 'Glass-Eye' (*na-gas-nelli*). Whenever I answered a question which I had misunderstood or only half-understood, everyone laughed loudly. I did what seemed to be the best thing and laughed along with them. After we had eaten and smoked a cigarette, the second part of the ceremony began. This time there was only singing. Sometimes they all sang together and sometimes they divided into two groups, as in the first part of the evening, and responded to each other; the music was not nearly so monotonous. The songs were quite merry and, I noticed, were interwoven with obscenities. 'Obscenities?' the reader asks, 'in the presence of women and children?'

"This is quite in accordance with Navaho custom. In the presence of women and children the Navahos will discuss the most improper things, which would be very much frowned upon in our society, but this company greeted each sally with pleasure and laughed heartily. I have even heard the women outdo the men in telling smutty stories, and yet their conduct was never criticized by the Indians.

"Hour after hour passed and there was no change in the proceedings. It was three o'clock in the morning, and Nature demanded her rights: Unable to keep my eyes open, I fell back in Morpheus' arms. This sleep didn't last long, for another kind of sleep awoke me—my legs had fallen asleep, and this reminded me that a soldier's bunk was a much better place to rest and that there I could stretch out and sleep much better than crouched in a crowded hogan. I went to my quarters and dreamed of medicine men painting each other, and cranes' heads threatening to devour a maiden, until the bugles sounded reveille.

"The following evening found me again in the Indian hut. I had learned about a sort of legend which is told in connection with the *noho-tschin-tchal*. I can't give all the details because my narrator spoke dreadful English and I worse Navaho. It was rather like a fairy tale: Once upon a time there were two brothers who went hunting together. Who the brothers were, what they were called, and to what tribe they belonged the narrator did not know, but he was certain they were not Navahos. The two men never returned. The people looked for them day after day without success. Two medicine men called a council; they spread out the buffalo robe and began to sing. It wasn't long before the heads of the two missing men rolled into the hut, making the same noise as the dried fawns' hooves, and landed on the buffalo robe. After a little while the two heads departed and the assembled company followed them. They came to a place in the mountains where the two brothers had been torn to pieces by a bear. The flesh had fallen from the bones and the coyotes had eaten some of it. They sang over the ants which were gathering up any of the flesh that was left. The medicine men now advised what to do. One of them, the one who healed, wanted to mix the remaining bits of flesh with black medicine and rebuild the bodies from that. The other medicine man objected to this idea, because, he said, the flesh of the Indian is red and not black.

"He went to work and made a paste of the flesh and red medicine. Out of this he made two bodies and put them on a deerskin which was spread over the buffalo robe. The wind, through an opening in the hut, blew into their bodies. They began to breathe and live. Since no one had thought to make muscles and sinews, the revived men could not raise themselves. Out of the rays of a rainbow (*na-zie-led*), muscles and sinews were belatedly created for them, which enabled the brothers to get up and walk. But they got no pleasure out of life. They were always ailing. The *noho-tschin-tchal* was instituted to keep them in good health—and if they haven't died, they are still happily living."

SIX

Shadow Catcher Mounts His Mule

URING his second enlistment, Christian Barthelmess served
at different times in the bands of both the Sixth Cavalry
and the Thirteenth Infantry, at Forts Wingate and Bayard, New
Mexico. Somehow, along with his military duties, he found time
to bring his photographic work into full bloom. Barthelmess took
pictures of soldiers in their post and field activities, of the Navaho, Zuñi, and Apache Indians in hogan, pueblo, and wickiup,
of the mesa home of the Hopis, and of people, places, and occasional events in some of the settlements near his post.

During this period also, Barthelmess took a wife. She was
Catherine Dorothea Hansen Ahlers, then twenty-three, nine
years younger than Barthelmess. Born in Flensburg, an industrial city of Schleswig-Holstein (then a part of Denmark), she
had come to America in 1881, under an arrangement by which
she accompanied the family of the German consul to Mexico,
with the understanding that she would reimburse the consul for
her passage by working for the family. After the obligation had
been met, she changed her residence to El Paso, Texas, where
she married John D. Ahlers, owner of a restaurant at Silver City,
New Mexico. They had one child. Ahlers owned mining interests
in Panama, and the family proceeded there, where he suc-
cumbed to fever. His wife and baby came back to New Orleans,
where the baby also died of fever. Mrs. Ahlers then returned
to Silver City. There, with the help of friends of her late husband, she opened a small café. And there she met Musician
Barthelmess, then with the Sixth Cavalry at Fort Bayard.[1] They
were married at Silver City on April 12, 1886.

[1] Fort Bayard, established in 1866 in southwestern New Mexico, was named

Barthelmess' second enlistment expired the following autumn. His discharge, dated November 14, 1886, bears, in addition to the conventional "Character: Excellent," the written notation, "A good musician and a good soldier." Barthelmess began his third enlistment December 2, 1886, and was assigned to the Twenty-second Infantry band at Fort Bayard. The Twenty-second had been organized in 1812; in 1815 it was consolidated with four other regiments. In 1861, the Twenty-second was organized again, this time as the Second Battalion of the Thirteenth Infantry, but in 1866 its identity as the Twenty-second was restored, and the Thirty-first was consolidated with it.

Within a year after Barthelmess joined the Twenty-second, the regiment was transferred from Fort Bayard to Fort Lewis, in southwestern Colorado, at the foot of the La Plata mountains. Units of the Twenty-second garrisoned Fort Lewis from 1882 to 1888. This fort was the second of two Colorado army posts bearing the name of Lieutenant Colonel William Henry Lewis, Nineteenth Infantry, who on September 28, 1878, died of wounds received the previous day in action against the Cheyennes on Punished Woman Creek in Kansas.[2] The first Fort Lewis was established in 1878 and garrisoned on October 17 of that year. It was near Pagosa Springs, where Indian and military trails crossed the San Juan River. Realignment of the Ute reservation necessitated relocation of the post, and a new site was chosen near Durango. There the second Fort Lewis was built in 1880 by men of the Thirteenth Infantry. The Fifteenth Infantry garrisoned the post until the autumn of 1882, when the Twenty-second took over.

Colonel Peter Tyler Swaine became commander of the Twenty-second and of Fort Lewis in April, 1884. Swaine, who was born in New York City, January 21, 1831, had a long and honorable army career. He entered West Point in 1847 and was

in honor of George Dashiell Bayard, a brigadier general of volunteers killed in the Civil War at the Battle of Fredericksburg. The fort was the center of operations against Apache bands led by Victorio and Geronimo.

[2] A graphic account of the engagement in which Lieutenant Colonel Lewis was killed is given from the Cheyenne point of view by Mari Sandoz in *Cheyenne Autumn*, Chapter 6, "A Soldier Chief Dead."

graduated in 1852; family tradition says he spent five years at the Academy, rather than the usual four, because in 1851 he was still so youthful looking that he was kept an extra year to mature. His first assignment was to the Tenth Infantry. In subsequent years he served with five other regular army regiments and the Ninety-ninth Ohio Volunteers. He was stationed in Texas, Utah, and Minnesota prior to the Civil War, was wounded at Stone River, and was brevetted colonel March 13, 1865. After duty in the South during Reconstruction, he served at Forts Wingate, Stanton, and Bayard, New Mexico, and then at Fort Lewis, Colorado, where he held command until 1888.[3]

The Twenty-second Infantry Band, in addition to playing on the base, occasionally made appearances at public affairs in neighboring towns. An orchestra was organized by the men of the regiment and played in Durango, on a stage in the dance hall, for a local talent production which was repeated at the fort. The comic opera thus presented was new at the time, having its *première* March 14, 1885, in London. It was the Gilbert and Sullivan classic, *The Mikado*.[4]

In Colorado, Barthelmess' trail was to take a new turn. His experiences were to widen, and a field-tested friendship was to be formed with a distinguished officer who was doomed to a tragic death. This friend was First Lieutenant Edward Wanton Casey, of California. Casey was a second generation West Pointer. He was graduated in 1873 and was assigned to the Twenty-second Infantry. He saw much frontier service, including participation in an encounter between forces of Colonel Nelson A. Miles and Lame Deer's band of Sioux, on May 7, 1877,

[3] Heitman, *Historical Register of the U.S. Army, 1789–1903*, I, 938; army records from National Archives; and manuscript (1937), "Memoirs of My Father and Mother," by Charles S. Swaine, one of Colonel and Mrs. Swaine's four children. The others were Edgar Lacy, William M., and Catherine Sophia Swaine. Catherine Sophia married Sherman Wallace Wiggins; their son, Wallace S. Wiggins, Whittier, California, possesses the manuscript referred to. Colonel Swaine died in 1904, his wife (the former Cornelia S. Lacy) in 1927, and Catherine Sophia in 1953.

[4] Mary C. Ayres, "History of Fort Lewis, Colorado," *The Colorado Magazine*, May, 1931, pp. 81–92.

on Muddy Creek, Montana, where Lieutenant Casey's conspicuous gallantry was officially recognized.[5]

While stationed at Fort Lewis, Lieutenant Casey became convinced of the army's need for better topographical and geographical knowledge of the country south and west, toward the Grand Canyon of the Colorado, in Arizona Territory, 450 miles from Fort Lewis. The Grand Canyon then was just beginning to be recognized as one of the country's great natural wonders. The gorge had first been seen by anyone other than Indians in 1540 when the Spanish explorer Cárdenas came upon it while seeking the Seven Cities of Cíbola. Mountain men and trappers had followed the Indian trails and had told of the "horrible" mountains that so hemmed in the river as to make it almost impossible of access. The United States government sent parties in during the 1850's and scientists began exploring it. An army man, Second Lieutenant Joseph Christmas Ives (who was born in New York and entered West Point from Connecticut but served throughout the Civil War with the Confederate Army), while a member of the Topographical Corps made an important exploration into the area 1857–58. The John Wesley Powell river expedition of 1869 put the Grand Canyon on the map, and by the early 1880's knowledge of its mineral wealth and geological marvels had begun to attract adventurous tourists. Early enterprisers developed roads and stage lines, writers and artists spread the word, and in 1902 the Canyon was designated as a National Monument. Eleven years later an area of more than one thousand square miles surrounding the canyon was set aside as a National Park.

But in 1887, Lieutenant Casey of the Twenty-second Infantry, dissatisfied with the knowledge of the area then available to the military, did something about it. On September 2, 1887, at Fort Lewis, Lieutenant Casey addressed the following letter through

[5] Heitman, *Historical Register of the U.S. Army, 1789–1903*, I, 289. General Miles, *Personal Recollections and Observations*, 250, describes the event: "The mounted infantry and scouts under Lieutenants Casey and [Lovell Hall] Jerome were ordered to charge directly up the valley and stampede the horses, while the battalion of cavalry followed at a gallop and attacked the camp. The command under Lieutenants Casey and Jerome stampeded the entire herd of ponies, horses and mules, and drove them five miles up the valley."

military channels to the Assistant Adjutant General, Department of the Missouri (Major General Alfred H. Terry commander), Fort Leavenworth, Kansas:

SIR: I have the honor to request that authority be granted me to make a trip from this post to the Grand Canyon of the Colorado River. My proposed route would be upon a right line drawn from the mouth of the La Plata River to the upper end of the Canyon, making such divergences as would enable me to visit one or two of the Moqui [Hopi] and Pueblo villages and also such detours as the nature of the country would of course render imperative. According to my information, no military itinerary has been made for the route I propose and the details of the country are not laid down upon any map I have ever seen. The country mentioned is in proximity to the reservations of the Navajo, Moqui and Pueblo Indians and for that reason some knowledge of the details might be of military interest. I would require for my outfit only such transportation and material as the Commanding Officer of the Post would see fit to furnish me, together with a few maps and instruments (odometers, barometers and compass) as I understand the Engineers Office of the Department will lend me. I would like to have two officers whose services the Post Commander can spare to accompany me, as their assistance would be necessary to the proper survey of the route. Also I would need a detachment of not to exceed six mounted men as escort. There will be no expense entailed upon the Government. If the Department Commander will grant my request I would leave the Post the latter part of this month or the first of October.

I am, Sir, very respectfully,

Your obedient servant,
E. W. CASEY, *1st Lieutenant*
22nd Infantry.[6]

The Lieutenant's assurance that the venture would entail no governmental expense was to be a costly one for him, as developments proved.

With endorsements, his letter was forwarded to Headquarters

[6] Records of the Office of the Adjutant General, Records Group 94, Regimental Returns 22nd Infantry, 1887. Other information used here is found in those records, and in A.G.O. Records Group 98, as well as in Register of Letters Received, 1887, Department of Missouri, Fort Leavenworth, all in the National Archives.

Indians from Picuris pueblo, N. M., give a Deer Dance in 1883 on a street in Santa Fe during the Tertio-Millenial Celebration of the founding of the city.

Zuñi pueblo, N. M., as Barthelmess saw it while stationed at Fort Wingate in 1882. Largest of the southwestern pueblos, it is the only inhabited one of seven ancient Zuñi towns, associated in history and legend with Coronado's Seven Cities of Cíbola.

Zuñi Mountain Sheep Dance, April 21, 1882. Barthelmess recorded the exact date of this picture, and added: "One of the most celebrated Indian events I ever saw."

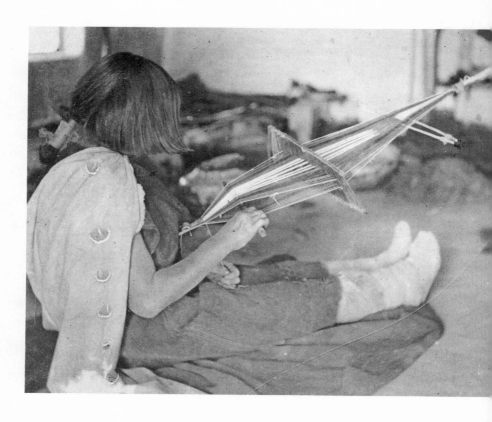

Zuñi woman weaving a belt.

Zuñi woman spinning yarn. Her style of dress—over the right shoulder and under the left—is typical Pueblo.

Barthelmess identified the woman in this portrait as the daughter of Mariana, Navaho war chief. It was made while he was stationed at Fort Wingate, in the early 1880's. A similar photograph of the young woman appears in Washington Matthews' "Navaho Legends" (*Memoirs of the American Folk-Lore Society*, 1897). Matthews says the woman is "Tanapa, who took her hair out of braid preparatory to standing before the camera."

Mariana's daughter, another portrait. She wears the traditional
Navaho blanket dress and leggings.

"Navaho woman mealing." The barefoot housewife is crushing grain, probably corn, on a metate, a flat stone on which the Indians of the Southwest and other areas, using a hand stone called a mano, pulverized maize, acorns, seeds, chile, and other foods.

"Navaho weaving one of those fine blankets. This one was made for Washington Matthews."—Barthelmess.

"The first Navaho scouts of A Troop, Fourth Cavalry, 1881."
Barthelmess identified the officer as Capt. Allen Smith.

Navaho hogan (of logs and mud) and its occupants. The man
rests his elbow on the entrance to the aboriginal habitation. His
wife, seated on his left, hides in her blanket, the top of her head
barely showing.

Ze-de-ke, a Navaho medicine man.

"Old Washy, a medicine woman of the Navahos and an old beggar around Fort Wingate. She was then (1883) supposed to be 106 years old."

A stop for water at Baker's Peak, Ariz. Of this picture, Barthelmess wrote: "Lt. Casey stands in the middle [just right of the water barrels]; to the left, Dr. Jarvis, a good man but a poor explorer. Farther back, Lt. Mosher."

This picture of the halt at Baker's Peak shows (left) the odometer (one-wheeled "contraption" drawn by a mule), which mea-
sured distance traveled.

Plaza at Walpi, one of the six Hopi villages in northeastern Arizona, photographed by Barthelmess in 1887 while on the Grand Canyon venture. Walpi was built high on a mesa for defensive purposes, accessible only by a ladder drawn up at night. Poles in the foreground mark one of the five Walpi kivas, subterranean sacred chambers, reached by ladders.

of the Army, at Washington, whence on September 24, 1887, word went back to the commanding officer of the Department of the Missouri that granting of the application was "left to his option." Eventually all hands cleared the matter, and on November 1, 1887, Orders No. 208, Fort Lewis, by direction of Colonel Swaine, gave the go-ahead and designated the personnel. The exploring party set out from Fort Lewis the following day.

Besides Casey, officers assigned to the expedition were First Lieutenant Theodore Mosher of G Company and Second Lieutenant F. B. Jones of K Company, Twenty-second Infantry. Enlisted men were Sergeants William Murphy, Charles Kieser, and Patrick Malone, Musician John Sullivan, and Privates Christian Barthelmess,[7] Hugo L. R. Lehman, Charles Reid, and Charles Morley. At the last minute, First Lieutenant Nathan S. Jarvis, an assistant army surgeon, was assigned to the group— fortunately. The unit was provided with seventy-five days' rations. Since this was more than could be packed on the mules, the post quartermaster, in addition to detailing two citizen packers and fifteen pack mules, provided a wagon as far as Fort Defiance. The wagon was, as it turned out, to become a source of considerable difficulty for Lieutenant Casey, and two of the soldiers—Privates Reid and Lehman—were to become casualties, Lehman in a diverting and somewhat unmilitary episode which bedeviled Casey in more ways than one.

In high spirits, the detachment departed from Fort Lewis November 2, 1887. On January 5, 1888, it wearily dragged itself back to the fort—mission accomplished, but at a considerable price in manpower and materials. It is to history's detriment that the full report of the Grand Canyon exploration is lost. There is, however, documentary evidence that on the journey Lieutenant Casey was afflicted with a series of misadventures beyond his power to control, and premonitory of the needless tragedy that three years later ended his career.

[7] Barthelmess was a noncommissioned officer both before and after this period, holding at various times the rank of corporal, sergeant, acting first sergeant, principal musician, and chief musician. He was listed as a private for his detached service on the Grand Canyon expedition.

Casey's original letter of September 2, 1887, asking authority to make the reconnaissance, and the approving documents, including Colonel Swaine's orders to proceed, are securely stored away among the old army records that have been concentrated in Washington in custody of the National Archives. There, too, is a brief report by Casey, written at Fort Lewis the day after his return, and forwarded through channels to Department of Missouri Headquarters, Fort Leavenworth. This communication says:

> SIR: I have the honor to inform you that I returned to this Post with my party yesterday evening from detached service authorized by Orders 208 from this Post. I made the Grand Canyon of the Colorado at a point ten miles below the mouth of the Little Colorado River. I was unable to make the north side of the Canyon owing to the snow on the Buckskin Mountains. My advance route was old Fort Defiance and Tuba City. My return was by way of Marsh's Pass and the northern end of the Canyon and mountains, practically making the right line specified in my application for authority for the expedition. I left one man at Ft. Defiance by reason of injury. This I reported. Another man was left at Cortez, Colorado, owing to serious injury from a fall. The remainder of my party returned in good health. I lost a number of animals on the way, from accidents and other causes unavoidable. Proper affidavits will be furnished the Quartermaster at this Post for all Government property lost. My report and maps of the route will be forwarded as soon as completed.
>
> Very respectfully,
>
> > Your obedient servant
> > E. W. CASEY, *1st Lieutenant*
> > *22nd Infantry.*

The report and maps referred to and thirty-five photographs taken on the expedition by Barthelmess were all duly filed. National Archives records show that Lieutenant Casey's full report, dated May 11, 1888, was received May 17 at the Engineers' Office, Department of Missouri. Accompanying it was a forwarding letter from Casey, saying that enclosed also were "field notes contained in blank books herewith; also the barometric record, which he [Casey] requests be given to Captain Whipple of the Ordnance Department, whose property it is, and stating that he will return by mail and express the instruments obtained from the Engineers Office, Department of Missouri. Map and photo views received separately."[8]

Unfortunately, the report, field notes, map, and photographs cannot now be found in the National Archives, though they once were there, nor have they been found as yet in other places in which they might somehow have been placed. Fortunately, Barthelmess himself preserved copies of some of the photographs in his personal album. Also, a fragment of Barthelmess' own felicitous description of the journey is still extant.

The brief report which Lieutenant Casey filed the day after his return to Fort Lewis, saying that he had returned but that two men had been injured and left behind, was "respectfully returned" to him the next day by the post adjutant, William H. Kell, on order of Colonel Swaine, the post commander. With the returned report was a brusque order for Casey to report in detail (the word *detail* underlined) on the accidents to the two men. In the case of the man left at Cortez, Colorado, Casey was to explain in full what arrangements had been made for the man's care and especially why he was turned over to a civilian doctor when Lieutenant Jarvis, an army surgeon, was with the expedition and it was "within the settlements and but forty miles from the Post." A list of property lost or destroyed, with a statement of the causes therefor, was also demanded.

Lieutenant Casey replied the next day with a fourteen-page letter written in strong, clear longhand. The wagon, he explained, had proved too light for effective duty, and its mule team unfit for strenuous service, so that the wagon had continually delayed the march. Casey had ordered the corporal in

---

[8] A.G.O., Records Group 98, file No. 1408, p. 203, May 17, 1888. The National Archives reported, December 30, 1963, that the Casey report was lost. It had been given file designation 2695 (A.G.O.) 1888, but was not filed there and has not been found, "despite an exhaustive search." That documents are sometimes lost in the vasty halls of the National Archives is not to be wondered at.

charge of the wagon to take it back to Fort Lewis, but the corporal had, after traveling eleven miles, left it with a man at Red Lake, 125 miles south of the San Juan River, and proceeded to the post without it. Of the pack mules, two were killed in an accident in the Grand Canyon, and two others gave out and were abandoned.[9] The men's mishaps were easily explained. Private Charles Reid's kneecap was fractured by a mule's kick. The soldier had been left at Fort Defiance in care of the physician at the Indian agency, who had taken the man into his own home. Arrangements had been made for his care and for his transport to the Fort Wingate hospital as soon as he could be moved. Private Lehman survived the perils of the thousand-mile journey through the Grand Canyon, the deserts, and Indian country, only to be severely injured near the end of the expedition—by falling down a well.

At the close of a day of hard traveling, the Casey contingent had come at dusk to the edge of a raw young Colorado settlement, called Cortez. Today, Cortez is a neat and thriving little city, gateway to Mesa Verde National Monument. In January, 1888, it was damp and dismal. The Casey expedition made camp at the edge of the town, in snow and mud. At a nearby livery stable, Lieutenant Casey bought grain and forage for his gaunt animals. Finding an empty store building near the stable, he arranged for the men to sleep there, while the officers spent the night in camp. After supper, Casey permitted the men to "go about the town," such as it was.

A well was being drilled at the intersection of the two dirt streets. Here a shaft five feet wide and sixty feet deep had been sunk and left unguarded, unmarked, and unlighted. In the dark, while returning to quarters, Private Lehman plunged to the bottom of the shaft. A crowd gathered, Casey and the other army officers were summoned from their camp, and a rope was

---

[9] The Fort Lewis post quartermaster, First Lieutenant John McA. Webster, requested that a Board of Survey be appointed to determine responsibility for the property loss and damage. This was standard military procedure, often resorted to for the sake of the record. Results of the inquiry in this case, if one was made, have not been found.

brought. Lieutenant Jones was lowered into the dark opening. He tied the rope to the fallen man, who, Casey's report said, then "was twisted out," carried to a drugstore and ministered to by Lieutenant Jarvis and "the local physician, a Dr. Williams." The doctors agreed that no one could determine the extent of the soldier's injury for several days but that he was obviously unfit to continue the march with his unit. Lieutenant Casey arranged for his care by the Cortez doctor, in a private home, at the Lieutenant's personal expense.[10]

The march toward home base was resumed the next day by the remainder of the men. They had but forty miles to go, but nearly half the distance was through the La Plata Mountains by way of a pass where snow was three feet deep. They were out of rations and their horses and mules were near exhaustion. The party traveled only eighteen miles in ten hours. Three of the men's feet froze. But they reached Fort Lewis.

"I do not see how I could have done otherwise than as I did under the circumstances," wrote Casey. "My duty was to the major part of my party, and to get it in in safety devolved upon me. Now that I have done it I am willing to return to the wounded man and either bring him back or stay with him. . . . I alone am responsible."

In some respects, Casey's experience in the Grand Canyon country in 1887 was similar to that of another army group one and one-half years later. In that instance, two officers of the Sixth Cavalry at Fort Defiance set out, with a Navaho scout and a civilian packer, on an off-duty junket to the Canyon, just to see it. They became separated and lost and wandered several days, suffering from thirst, heat, and exhaustion, in the desert between Tuba City and the Grand Canyon. Eventually reunited, the four men made their way to the Canyon and back to Fort Defiance. One of the two officers involved in this episode was Second Lieutenant John M. Stotsenburg, who in 1899

[10] Cortez, seat of Montezuma County, was founded in 1886 by the Montezuma Land and Development Company. "Ed Lamb had the first drugstore in Cortez . . . . The first doctor was young Dr. Williams."—*The Colorado Magazine,* July, 1940, p. 137, and July, 1935, p. 156.

was killed in action against Aguinaldo *insurrectos* in the Philippines. The other was Second Lieutenant John J. Pershing, then twenty-nine, who lived to become America's six-starred General of the Armies in World War I.[11]

[11] Under the title "Lt. John J. Pershing at the Grand Canyon," *Montana: The Magazine of Western History*, April, 1963, pp. 11–23, Donald Smythe describes Pershing's adventure, basing his account on Stotsenburg's diary and Pershing's unpublished autobiography, in the Pershing Papers, Library of Congress. Also, in "Lieutenants Pershing and Stotsenburg Visit the Grand Canyon: 1887," *Arizona and the West*, Autumn, 1961, pp. 265–84, William Swilling Wallace prints Stotsenburg's account of the trip from the original manuscript. Stotsenburg thus refers to the expedition in which Christian Barthelmess took part: "We determined, after consulting with several who had been a long while in the country, not to take the usual route, but to cross the Little Colorado south of the Mormon town of Tuba City, and then travel a little west of south to the point where Lieutenant Casey and a detachment from Fort Lewis had gone into the canyon the previous fall."

SEVEN

"With Song and Bell"

SOME TIME after his return from the Grand Canyon, Musician Barthelmess wrote in German his own account of that adventure. His longhand manuscript, undated, was found after his death in 1906. He apparently had intended to submit the article to the Chicago newspaper that had printed his two accounts of experiences among the Navahos, for on the first page he wrote: "*Für den Westen.*" Why he did not send it to the newspaper, or whether he did so and it was returned, nobody knows. His widow kept the manuscript for years, but somehow it became lost, except for the opening pages, which are now in possession of Casey Barthelmess.

The existing fragment of the manuscript takes Lieutenant Casey's expedition through the first few days of its outward journey. It is tantalizingly incomplete, but gives a humorous and spirited account of what Barthelmess saw, in retrospect, as an enterprise of what was sometimes a "clumsy and stupid" army. It is also revelatory of the descriptive talents and cultural background of the "Shadow Catcher" from Bavaria. His unfinished story follows:[1]

"Paul Lindau gave the readers of his 'The West' in the year 1883 an interesting description of what he had seen in the Grand Canyon of the Colorado.[2] The Atlantic-Pacific railroad brought him within twenty-five miles of the Canyon, but my colleagues and I had to travel on Government mules for 450 long and tire-

---

[1] Translated in 1938 by Arthur W. Wirch, an American of German descent, then in the U.S. Forest Service at Miles City, Montana. This fragment of Christian Barthelmess' writings appeared in *The Denver Westerners' Brand Book for 1953*. It is reprinted here by permission of The Westerners.

[2] Paul Lindau was a German playwright, novelist, journalist, and editor (1839–1919).

some miles merely to enable us to look into the Canyon from above. Naturally, I cannot offer my readers anything in the style of Lindau; but if they have leisure to give attention to the notes and photographs of one whose lot happened to be that of a musician in the American army, it shall be of the greatest satisfaction to me and I shall try my best in what follows to acquaint my readers with the region and its inhabitants.

"The War Department had given permission to a number of officers at Fort Lewis, Colorado, to conduct a military reconnaissance for the purpose of improving and correcting existing maps of the Grand Canyon of the Colorado, and, after manifold and various preparations and arrangements, most of which subsequently proved insufficient or worthless, the reconnaissance party started out from Fort Lewis on the 2nd of November, 1887.

"The party included the three Lieutenants, Casey, Mosher and Jones, of the Twenty-second Infantry, in whom the four temperaments were represented with exceptional completeness and whose regulations and orders too often reminded us of Solon the Citizen-Soldier, Mrs. Spoopendyke, and the *Jobsiade*.[3]

"For our physical well-being we had Dr. Jarvis, an army doctor whose ill-fortune it had been to be removed from Bellevue Hospital in paradise-like New York and cast into the deserts of New Mexico and Arizona.

"Other than these, our company consisted of Non-Commissioned Officers Murphy, Malone and Kieser and Privates Reid, Morley, Sullivan, Barthelmess and Lehman, and two packers.

"We were all mounted. The officers, with the exception of the doctor, had their own mounts. The other members of the company were armed with Government mules.

"Most of my readers no doubt are acquainted with the com-

---

[3] The ancient Greek concept of the Hippocratic school of medicine was that the human temperament was determined by the four "humours" or fluids conceived of as existing in the body, resulting in temperaments sanguine, phlegmatic, melancholic, or choleric. Modern physiology has grown beyond acceptance of this theory for categorizing human beings, but it was still valid in Barthelmess' day. Solon, the Athenian statesman and "founder of democracy," was born *ca.*638 B.C. He was one of the Seven Sages of ancient Greece. Barthelmess apparently likened Lieutenant Casey to Solon. The *Jobsiade* was a popular comic epic by K. A. Kartum, a German writer (1745–1824).

mon, everyday mule, *Mulus communis*, as he is found roaming throughout the Western states, and know how, in case of total absence of his regular diet, he can subsist on fence posts, barbed wire, old tin cans, newspapers and theater tickets. A Government mule, however, *Mulus governmentalis*, has a social standing in the mule world as far above that of the common mule as a Congressman is above the layman. Thus the reader will know what a Company of Korah[4] of mules we had to deal with. This will give him a better understanding of our quiet, innocent suffering, so that the reader may not blame us too much for our frequent perversions of the Christian Catechism.

"Eighteen pack mules and eleven saddle mules, with the cussedness common to both common and Government mules, thus left behind them the flesh-pots of the Egyptians for the sake of making their braying re-echo in the Grand Canyon of the Colorado. And all of these mules, my Daisy excepted, were conscious of the in-born electric power of their hind legs, specifically, that mysterious power which strikes a person like an individual earthquake and sends him by first-class ticket to the Great Beyond, whence any further observation of Government mules is possible only from a bird's-eye view.

"As long as a Government mule remains at a military post, he belongs to that preferred class which invests a public office: he is an office-holder in the fullest sense of the word, in that his manger is filled twice a day. And for this he will perform only as much service as becomes the dignity of the long-eared quadruped office-holder that he is.

"When the mule goes into the field, his rations are reduced one half; gradually, by necessity, they are reduced to quarter-ration, and then finally the last particle of corn has become but a memory, and by this time the Government mule feels like a Congressman whose district did not re-elect him. He—the mule, not the Congressman—now considers himself on a level with the common mule. His last vestige of meekness disappears, and if one must handle such mules several times daily for a couple of

---

[4] In the Bible, Korah was a Levite who led a rebellion against Moses and Aaron. His descendants, the Korahites, were temple musicians.

months, there are numberless times when one has one foot in the grave, never knowing when the hind leg of his mule will be transformed into the Angel of Death. So much for the Government mule. Should you ever attend an auction, and should an earthquake and a Government mule be offered for sale, and should you feel an inner urge to buy something tremendous, buy the earthquake; it needs not to be fed, does not bray, and has no hind legs.

"The American army, even here in the West, is in some respects clumsy and stupid, and so the procession of 29 mules and 14 mounted men planned to start early so that the entire retinue could make its getaway in one day. It was, however, four o'clock in the afternoon before everything was packed and everyone mounted, and the Regimental Quartermaster, the Adjutant and many others, to whom our preparations and equipping had become the bane of their existence, wished us farewell at the gates of the Post. With song and bell, and in the rosy spirits that allow one to think kindly even of one's mother-in-law, we started out in the direction of the river La Plata.

"Three miles south of the Post we made our first camp. This was so that everything could be checked out and those articles that might have been overlooked, and which actually were overlooked, after our three weeks of preparation, could still be procured.

"That evening the Regimental Band came out, also a number of officers, and offered us a first-class serenade. [Here, says the translator, Barthelmess inserted the German phrase for "Eat, drink and be merry for tomorrow you may die."]

"The next morning everyone felt as if he had been an active participant in a boiler explosion. The mules, which had been tied up during the night, also showed definite signs of pessimistic spirits. Nothing seemed to be as it should be. In spite of this, we were on the march by eight o'clock.

"Every hour we 'made a station' for a five-minute pause in which we maltreated the thermometer, barometer, odometer and other meters with which we were outfitted, to observe the clouds, wind and country, the resulting observations all being entered with solemn faces in the books. This was done with as exacting care as if the specific security of the United States and general welfare of the rest of the universe depended upon it.

"Of all the instruments we had with us, the odometer was the greatest white elephant. [The author calls it "pitchfowl," which is the German equivalent.—Translator.] This instrument is a simple arrangement of two metal discs mounted on the same concentric shaft and graduated in degrees, one having 99 gradations and the other 100, the latter being actuated by friction as it bears against the wagon wheel. [In simpler language, an odometer is an instrument used to measure distance; what the author describes is the vernier, with which the particular instrument used on this trip was supplied, a scale for indicating parts of divisions.]

"The contraption is absolutely shapeless so long as it rests in its case. I always thought it should have a 'Don't meddle, don't touch' sign on it. It may be used without serious misgivings on an ordinary wagon, for a wagon rests on its four wheels. But in the case of the new-fangled vehicle we used, which issued from the Patent Office in Washington, the odometer felt entirely out of place and showed evidence of the highest degree of impatience.

"Picture, if you will, a heavy wheel, four feet in diameter and equipped with shafts, to which was hitched the largest mule. This mule was covered with more than thirty yards of straps, leather and harness which kept him completely confused when he tried to pull the 'bad luck cart.' In addition to all this, he carried a saddle and wore a bridle to accommodate a spurred rider. Each of us, with the exception of Lehman—who must at some time have walked through the house of a mathematician and was therefore sentenced to calculate the readings of the odometer—alternately rode the mule, and I was naturally the first to give the thing a trial.

"But I had no luck. The wheel tipped to the right side, then to the left, and sometimes, I am sure, to both sides at the same time. This occasioned considerable adjustment of strap and harness. Professional opinions were aired, and advice followed. The whole contraption was even wished to the devil, but the wheel went serenely on as before, first to one side and then to the other. Everyone lavished his compassion on the mule. By the end of the second day, we could tell by the expression on his face that he was begging to be excused from living.

"For two days we traveled over dusty trails in the direction of the river La Plata. Our destination was Farmington [New Mexico], a miserable collection of dreary sod houses, in which a handful of people struggled for an existence.

"The expedition had been supplied at the post with 75 days' rations, but, even with considerable strangling and cinching, the mules could be loaded with only 15 days' provisions, so the balance had been piled into a Government wagon, drawn by six mules and guarded by six cavalrymen, which followed in our rear. The driver of this wagon was named Shorty.

"Shorty had been a muleskinner in most of the army posts of New Mexico, Arizona, Texas, Dakota and Montana, and he knew the sizes and shapes of each of these states and territories and was known and feared in each of them only as Shorty. His real name he kept in the darkest secrecy and no one troubled to lift the veil of this secrecy, for the name Shorty was sufficient for all ordinary purposes in the Western country. It is quite possible he received the name because of his curt nature. Closer examination and observation of 'the short one,' however, coupled with some speculative reflection, gave me the impression that he might have deserved the name because he was always short on soap, towels and water. Washing of the hands and face belonged to those vices to which Shorty was addicted only on the Fourth of July and, perhaps, on New Year's Day.

"On one night, during which we had a torrential rain that washed us out of our camp, in which Shorty received an involuntary bath that he tried to shake off at the camp fire, I pried far enough into his confidence to discover that this nondescript assemblage of natural and territorial acquisitions was of German descent, and that he understood German very well and spoke it . . . though of course not with much pretense at purity.

"Shorty and his wagon were a complete Westinghouse air

brake[5] to our flying expedition. Whenever we would become a little enthusiastic and travel on apace with high hope in our breasts, one of the cavalrymen would overtake us with the news that the wagon had become hopelessly mired down some six or eight miles back, and that the muleskinner was in dire need of our assistance. Twice did we send our packers and pack mules back to relieve Shorty and his air brake of their burden and float them again. After reaching Farmington, where a blacksmith earned fifty cents for repairs to Shorty's wagon, he and his caravan were sent by way of the wagon roads to Fort Defiance, Arizona, while we took off at a tangent, through brush and over Indian trails, for the same destination, happy in the belief that we were finally rid of the wagon.

"Not far from Farmington we forded the San Juan river, at that point a small but swift stream of some one hundred feet width, and found ourselves on the Navaho Indian reservation. Rock Springs was our next objective, for if one travels in the deserts of Arizona and New Mexico he is required to keep his eye first on water, next on grass, and finally on fuel, if he does not wish to come to grief. Rock Springs was our nearest water, but whether we would be able to find grass and fuel there only the gods knew. For twelve lonely miles we rode onward over an Indian trail, while trees, bushes, weeds and grass gradually vanished behind us, and finally we found ourselves in the alkali deserts of New Mexico. This geological feature seemed to be of volcanic origin, for Nature has here tried in vain to grow even a spear of grass on the dead, scorched, barren, cold soil. The alternating and disturbing action of rain and burning sun had transformed the upper layers of this lifeless desert into a finely sculptured mosaic that shimmered in the sunlight with all the colors of the rainbow. Red was predominant. Our jaded mules sank up to their knees with every step. The desert on which Sodom and Gomorrah once stood[6] must present the same dreary and forsaken picture today.

[5] The Westinghouse air brake had been patented about twenty years before this expedition fared forth.

[6] They were destroyed "with fire and brimstone" (Genesis 19: 24).

"Here the scouts, who preceded us in a semi-circle, in spite of all the maps and topographic sketches they had with them, showing ten different roads and trails, chose and followed with utter confidence the only wrong route existing, and this day it was again deep twilight before we arrived at Rock Springs. We found very little grass. The water had a strong alkali taste. The wood for our fire we had to get down from a jagged hogback.

"Our meals on the journey invariably consisted of bread, bacon, and coffee. A sampling of beans, cooked and baked under great difficulties and seasoned with desert sand, was like the bright rays of the sun in our diet heaven, everlastingly overcast as it was by bread-and-bacon clouds. In Rock Springs we rested for twenty-four hours and cooked up a batch of sunbeams while waiting for our wagon, which was again to cross our path at this point.

"Shorty, with the uncanny powers of finding things that characterized him, had this time found a really soft spot in a dry stream bed nine miles away, in which he was deeply mired. The courier sent out by him brought us the . . . ."

And there that record ends.

From his detached service with the reconnoitering party, Musician Barthelmess was returned to the Twenty-second Infantry band. Within a short time, the Twenty-second was transferred to Fort Keogh, Montana, being replaced as the garrison at Fort Lewis by units of the Sixth Cavalry and the Sixth Infantry, under command of Major Tullius Cicero Tupper of the Sixth Cavalry. The Twenty-second departed from Fort Lewis April 12, 1888; traveling via Fort Lyon, Colorado, it arrived at Fort Keogh on June 6. Colonel Swaine became post commander.

Musician Barthelmess was sick in quarters for a week that summer, with a case of "sore lips, contracted in line of duty." Fort Keogh was to be his station for the rest of his military service, and his residence as a civilian after retirement. It was at Keogh that all his children except the oldest were born. There Barthelmess continued his association with Lieutenant Casey, and there he did some of his best camera work.

EIGHT

New Fort on the Yellowstone

Montana's Fort Keogh, had it been named in a mood matching that which wrote into American history such place names as Fort Necessity, Fort Recovery, and Fort Defiance, might have been called Fort Deferred. As early as 1873 army officers fighting the hostile Northern Plains Indians had beseeched Congress for funds with which to establish a strong base of operations in the 90,000-square-mile habitat of their elusive and dangerous quarry. But 1873 was a year of national financial panic, as depressions were then called. The officers' pleas went into pigeonholes; Congress saved money, and the army lost lives. Not until 260 men had been shoveled into shallow graves on the banks of the Little Big Horn did the lawmakers act. Hurriedly, then, on July 22, 1876, Congress authorized the new post that had been so long deferred.

Before the post could be built, the Indians won a couple of battles, but in the long run the army won the war. Fort Keogh stood for three decades as one of victory's bastions, protecting the border and training troops for future frontiers far from the Yellowstone Valley.

On the Southern Plains by the middle 1870's the Indian barrier to the westward surge of white settlement had been eliminated by the military conquest of the Comanches, Kiowas, and Southern Cheyennes and their confinement on reservations. On the Northern Plains the Sioux and Northern Cheyennes in large numbers were still defiant, although some had given up and accepted their fate as agency Indians. The Indian Bureau in Washington in 1875 estimated the total number of malcontents or so-called hostiles off the reservations in the north at approximately three thousand. Their warriors were well armed and mounted, and were led by such desperate and bitter irreconcilables as Sitting Bull and Crazy Horse of the Sioux, and Dull Knife and Little Wolf of the Cheyennes.

Since 1849 the Indian tribes had been under the civilian jurisdiction of a commissioner of Indian affairs who was responsible to the secretary of the interior. This setup was originally full of what the road to hell is paved with, but had become so riddled with politics, inefficiency, and dishonesty that good intentions, by the time they were translated into action on the distant reservations, usually did more harm than good, as far as achieving anything by way of "civilizing" the Indians was concerned. When crises arose, standard operating procedure was to take the problem out of civilian hands and turn it over to the military, usually too late and with too little means to achieve any immediate solution but a blood bath.

The Sioux and their Cheyenne allies had in the 1860's forced the government to close the Bozeman Road, which ran from the Oregon Trail in Wyoming to the Montana gold fields, and to abandon Fort Phil Kearny and other northern posts. They had slaughtered eighty-one of Lieutenant Colonel W. J. Fetterman's men, and they had inflicted casualties at the Hayfield and Wagonbox fights. Small-scale fighting broke out sporadically. Gold was found in the Black Hills in 1874, and the rush of prospectors fed the fires of resentment and hate. Wagon trains were attacked and settlements raided.

To handle the Sioux and Cheyennes, the regular army in 1876 could muster in the area about 7,500 officers and men—174 companies, of varying strength—stationed at more than a score of small forts, headquarters, depots, and Indian agencies in Wyoming, Montana, and Dakota Territory. Based on small, undermanned, and widely separated posts, the army units in the field operated on long and tenuous lines of communication and supply. From Fort Abraham Lincoln in Dakota, Custer's men marched more than three hundred miles to the Little Big Horn. General George Crook led his forces nearly as far, from Fort

Crow Indian scaffold burial, near Custer Battlefield, 1890.

Crow Indian camp on ground now occupied by East Billings, Mont. Yellowstone River flows at foot of the distant bluffs.

Fort Keogh bakery, about 1891.

Soap Suds Row home of Sgt. Tackelberry, Twenty-second Infantry, one of the early log homes at Fort Keogh. Most western posts had areas called Soap Suds Row because many enlisted men's wives laundered for their own and officers' families. The shack in rear of this home housed the family water barrels.

Written on this photograph: "My school, November, 1892. Laura
G. Ritner." She conducted the school for children of Fort Keogh
personnel.

Chris Barthelmess studio under construction, 1890. Mrs. Barthelmess on right, holding Florence; beside her, Eliza Griffin, who later married John Kelly, post saddler; Leo Barthelmess, second from left, with Q. M. Sgt. Moran on roof at right.

Fort Keogh, 1896, looking southwest, with Sgt. Woods, Second Infantry, and his trusty bicycle. Three-chimneyed building left is guardhouse; large building right center, band quarters; then the post headquarters, with regimental headquarters building in its rear; officers' quarters on right. Center, steam engine, left standing in place after the sawmill which housed it burned to the ground, used for cutting fireplace cordwood into shorter lengths for stoves.

The last Cantonment No. 1 on Tongue River, near its junction with the Yellowstone, southeastern Montana. Apparently when Christian Barthelmess came to Fort Keogh in 1888 with the Twenty-second Infantry, this much of the old cantonment was still standing, although in process of demolition.

Yellowstone River ferryboat, west of Fort Keogh. "Lt. Peter Davidson with detachment off on a survey."—Barthelmess.

Squad room, L Troop, Sixth Cavalry, about 1900. Poster at far
end advertises Iron Worker cigars.

Post exchange at Fort Keogh, 1890. From left, Chris Barthelmess; Lt. Robert N. Getty, Twenty-second Infantry; unidentified soldier; William Griffin, clerk.

Fort Keogh officers' quarters, winter, 1893.

A Troop, Tenth Cavalry, Colored (guidon left), with sabers drawn, cavalry stables and piles of cordwood in the rear. Capt. Cooper, center; to his left, two trumpeters—on gray horses. At this period, the army still had two Negro cavalry regiments, the Ninth and the Tenth, both organized in 1866 with white officers.

Twenty-second Infantry firing prone at long-range targets on the rifle range half a mile north of Fort Keogh, using Springfield rifles, about 1890. Dark mass extending from left over half of the picture, beyond the long pile of cordwood, is the haystack for cavalry and quartermaster stock.

The Twenty-second Infantry leaves Fort Keogh in 1896, by train.
It had come to Keogh in 1888 to relieve the Fifth Infantry, which
had arrived in 1876 by steamboat.

Members of M Troop, Sixth Cavalry, Fort Keogh, model types of uniform in 1904, when olive drab replaced the old blue uniform that had served through the Indian wars. From left, standing: Sgt. Harry Chartran in new olive drab overcoat with head cover attached; Corp. Hunker in summer khaki such as was used in the Philippines; Pvt. Vessay in "the last of the blues"; unidentified soldier in winter garb, blanket-lined heavy canvas overcoat, muskrat cap, one-finger mittens and buckle overshoes; seated, the old dress blues and the new olive drab, wearers unidentified.

Fetterman in Wyoming, to take a beating from Crazy Horse on the Rosebud in Montana, June 17, 1876.

Lieutenant General Philip H. Sheridan, commanding the Division of the Missouri, in 1873 recommended erection of "a large military post near the base of the Black Hills, at some point to be selected hereafter. In this way we could secure a strong foothold in the heart of the Sioux country and thereby exercise a controlling influence over these warlike people." He repeated his request in 1874 and 1875, altering it to the extent of asking for two "permanent and large" new posts on the Yellowstone, one at the mouth of the Tongue and one on the Big Horn. William T. Sherman, general of the army, supported the recommendations.

However, Congress paid more attention to those who said that the Indians were only rattling their lances—that they posed no serious threat. The Indian commissioner in 1875 assured the Secretary of the Interior that there could be no war, because the hostile bands could bring but a few hundred fighting men into the field. An inspector in the Indian country in November, 1875, confirmed the opinion that war rumors were unfounded, but did recommend that all Sioux and Cheyennes who were not then on reservations be compelled to go there.

By telegraph and courier, then, the Secretary of the Interior sent word to Sitting Bull and Crazy Horse and other leaders of hostile bands—"these desperadoes," Commissioner J. Q. Smith called them—to bring their followers in to the agencies by January 31, 1876. This ultimatum was an almost meaningless gesture except that it put the government publicly on record to help justify a war which some historians believe the administration in Washington (U. S. Grant was President) had already decided upon as necessary to complete the process, prolonged over a period of years and through a series of treaties, of taking the Sioux hunting lands away piecemeal.

Out on the plains, the demand that the angry red sons of the wild wind give up their ways, and what they considered their land, filtered through with little impact. No realist could have expected that the Indians would suddenly come in, settle down, and be good just because they were told to do so by some words on a piece of paper.

So, on February 1, 1876, the off-reservation Indians were figuratively dumped in the army's lap. The military was ordered to enforce the civilian ultimatum. Troops took the field in the war that couldn't happen, with the Sioux and their allies reaching the peak of their military prowess at the Little Big Horn, where they destroyed Custer with perhaps ten times as many warriors as the Indian commissioner had naïvely set as their maximum fighting strength.

Thus jolted, Congress pulled the generals' recommendations from their pigeonholes and within a month passed a special appropriation of $200,000 to build two forts along the Yellowstone. General Sherman lost no time in recriminations, though he did, in his 1876 report, recall the futility of his previous pleas and those of General Sheridan; and Sheridan could not restrain an "I-told-you-so." "Had my advice been taken," he said in his report, "there would have been no war." Then the generals went on with their job of getting the now scattered hostiles, flushed with victories, off their war horses and on the reservations.

Building of the two new forts was a first step. One was to be on the major tributary of the Yellowstone, the Big Horn, some thirty miles upstream from its mouth. The site was near the point where the Big Horn is joined by the Little Big Horn, close to the present Montana city of Hardin. This post was built and garrisoned within the year and named Fort Custer. It served well in the next few years, until 1890, when it was abandoned.

The other new fort was to be on the mighty Yellowstone, largest tributary of the mightier Missouri. The Yellowstone rises in the mountains of Yellowstone National Park and flows northeastward across Montana. It forms part of the water highway followed through the wilderness by Lewis and Clark and other early explorers, trappers, and mountain men.

Commercial navigation by steamboat on the Missouri had begun in 1830, and in ensuing decades the little stern-wheel, wood-burning, shallow-draft steamers played dramatic roles in the development of the Northwest. Since 1859, the head of navigation on the Missouri had been Fort Benton, located 2,285 miles above the mouth of the Missouri and about forty miles northeast of Great Falls, Montana. How far the Yellowstone was navigable, however, had not been proved until 1875, when General Sheridan ordered it explored to determine whether steamboats could use it to take materials, supplies, and men to his base on the Yellowstone, when and if the fort was built. To make the exploration, Sheridan had sent his military secretary, Lieutenant Colonel James W. Forsyth.[1] On the steamboat *Josephine*, Captain Grant Marsh, pilot and master, the Forsyth party had embarked early in May, 1875, to study the timber, soil, and geological formations of the stream, as well as its depth and the character of the current. The group included scientists from the Smithsonian Institution, seven officers and one hundred men of the Sixth Infantry, and four scouts and hunters headed by Lonesome Charley Reynolds, who died the next year with Custer. Captain Marsh pushed the *Josephine* upstream from the mouth of the Yellowstone (near the northeastern corner of Montana) 483 miles to Pompey's Pillar, a Lewis and Clark landmark about one hundred miles from the present Yellowstone National Park. On his return, Forsyth reported the Yellowstone navigable to the Big Horn, twenty-five miles downstream from Pompey's Pillar.[2]

But in the fall of 1876 low water and the approach of winter made it impossible to get to the Keogh site the materials that had been rushed up the Missouri to the mouth of the Yellowstone. There the materials awaited spring, when the ice would be gone and runoff water from the mountain snows would raise the stream level and open the river to traffic. General Sheridan ordered interim establishment of a temporary post, or canton-

[1] The two generals named Forsyth were brothers. James William Forsyth, West Point 1855, the one who explored the Yellowstone in 1875, later commanded the Seventh Cavalry at Wounded Knee. General George Alexander ("Sandy") Forsyth rose from the ranks. He commanded the scouts who fought the Cheyenne Roman Nose (Bat) in 1868 on the Arikaree River, Colorado. Each Forsyth served in the Civil War as well as on the western frontier, and each was, at a different time, military aide to General Sheridan.

[2] Joseph Mills Hanson, *The Conquest of the Missouri*, chap. XXV, "Bound for the Mountains."

ment, on the Yellowstone at the mouth of the Tongue, to be garrisoned that year by Colonel Nelson A. Miles and the Fifth Infantry.

Thus, in August, 1876, there came into being Fort Keogh's progenitor, a camp of tents and huts—a primitive and transitory military installation which in its short existence was designated in official orders and military communications by a variety of names. These ranged from the short and simple "Tongue River, M.T.," to "Headquarters, Troops on Yellowstone River, Montana Territory, Cantonment at Tongue River." On some contemporary documents it was shown as "Post on Tongue River." On some it was called "Yellowstone Command, Post No. 1, M.T." There were other variations, such as "Tongue River Barracks" and "New Post on the Yellowstone."[3]

The Fifth Infantry was stationed at Fort Leavenworth, Kansas, when it was ordered to what Miles called "that 'dark and bloody ground,'" the Yellowstone Valley. At first, Lieutenant Colonel Joseph Nelson Garland Whistler, a West Pointer who had served in the Mexican War, was given command of the six companies ordered to the new post. Colonel Miles pointed out to his superiors that as six companies constituted more than half his regiment, he himself should have command, and it was so ordered. Subsequently the rest of the regiment followed the first units to Montana. By foot, train, and steamboat the six companies moved to the Yellowstone in late summer of 1876, passing at times through cheering settlements whose excitement over the Indian war recalled to Miles the stirring days of 1861. Towns were draped with black for Custer and with the Stars and Stripes for reinforcements moving to the front. The command moved up the Missouri to the Yellowstone, up the Yellowstone to the Rosebud, and up the Rosebud to a junction with forces already in the field commanded by Generals Alfred H. Terry and George Crook. Terry's forces had been shaken in the Custer campaign, Crook's in his debacle at the Rosebud. The combined forces moved east to the mouth of the Powder River,

[3] Fort Keogh documents, 1876–77, in the Casey E. Barthelmess Collection, Miles City, Montana.

where they again separated, Crook going into temporary camp near the Dakota Black Hills, Terry eastward and downriver to other stations, leaving in the Yellowstone area only the Fifth Infantry and six companies of the Twenty-second—no cavalry.[4]

Lieutenant Colonel Whistler had charge of selecting the site for Tongue River Cantonment No. 1, and of constructing the temporary buildings that comprised that outpost. The work began on August 28, with such materials as could be obtained in the area, supplemented by some brought overland in wagons. The site was on the south side of the Yellowstone and the west side of the Tongue, in the angle formed by their confluence, where a little shelter from the wind was afforded by the river bluffs and a cottonwood grove.

Cottonwood poles set on end, stockade style, formed the walls of the huts that served as barracks. The poles were sunk into a trench, chinked with mud, and topped with horizontal logs on which rested a roof of poles and earth. There was one exception: Colonel Miles's headquarters was made of squared logs laid horizontally. Some of the men who occupied the cantonment that first winter spoke of it as being dark, dismal, and vermin-infested. But Colonel Miles was proud of the place and the speed with which it had been built. The mud chinking and dirt roofs melted in heavy rains and ran down the walls, yet the structures were warm enough for the use that was made of them. The troops quartered there were in the field much of the winter that the cantonment was used.[5]

The site for the permanent fort, as chosen by Miles, was officially described as "situated on the right bank of the Yellowstone River, two miles above the mouth of the Tongue . . . on a solid elevation about ten feet above the remainder of the Yellowstone and Tongue River bottom . . . altitude 2,530 feet above sea level . . . area of reservation about 90 square miles."

In 1877, as the "spring rise" brought the Yellowstone up to a

[4] Nelson A. Miles, *Personal Recollections*, 212ff.

[5] Miles, *Personal Recollections*; *Annual Reports* of the Secretary of War; Fort Keogh records in the National Archives; Mari Sandoz, *Cheyenne Autumn*; and Virginia Weisel Johnson's *The Unregimented General: A Biography of Nelson A. Miles*, are sources for much of the information in this chapter.

navigable level, the finishing lumber, doors, windows, shingles, hardware, and other materials for the fort buildings came by steamboat from the mouth of the Yellowstone, where they had waited out the winter. With them came artisans to help with the construction job. The river shipments were supplemented by overland wagon trains, and sawmills buzzed in the pine hills.

The new post was informally known as Fort Keogh from the time of its inception, but the name did not become official until November 8, 1878. In naming the post, the army paid tribute to Captain Myles Walter Keogh, of I Troop, Seventh Cavalry, who had died with Custer.

Keogh was born in 1840, in Ireland, the son of a Royal Irish Lancer whose station was in a town near Limerick known by a name now forever associated with the Seventh Cavalry—"Garry Owen." Miles Keogh served in the French and Italian armies and in the Papal Zouaves before coming in 1862 to America, where he volunteered for the Union Army. He was mustered-out in 1866 as a brevet lieutenant colonel, re-enlisted, and ten years later was killed by the Indians. It was Captain Keogh's horse, Comanche, which was found alive on the Little Big Horn battlefield, nursed back to health despite his seven wounds, and was thus enabled to live for fifteen years to be preserved as an exhibit in the museum at the University of Kansas, at Lawrence.

To the Northern Cheyennes, who had long used the Fort Keogh site as a camping ground and whose name for the Yellowstone was Elk River, the new installation was known as the Elk River Fort.

The fort was an eleven-company post, and building it was costly. The Quartermaster General's report to the Secretary of War for 1877 predicted that the expense of transporting materials to the site would "much exceed" costs of construction and materials. This apparently did not prove to be the case, but transportation was the largest of the three items, and the amount spent on Fort Keogh alone in two years nearly equaled the entire $200,000 originally appropriated in 1876 for Forts Keogh and Custer.

The Quartermaster General's report for 1877 listed the following buildings for Keogh with the "expected cost" of each:

Two cavalry barracks for six companies	$ 20,800.00
Two infantry barracks for four companies	10,000.00
One infantry barrack for one company	3,000.00
One building as quarters for commander	3,300.00
Thirteen buildings, company and staff officers	39,000.00
One commissary warehouse	2,500.00
One quartermaster storehouse	2,200.00
One bake house	1,000.00
Stables and corral for cavalry horses	10,000.00
Stables and corral for trains	2,000.00
Office of commander	2,000.00
Guard house	2,000.00
Granary for forage	2,200.00
	————————
	$100,000.00

There is in the National Archives a scale drawing, marked "Plan of Fort Keogh, M.T.," prepared under direction of First Lieutenant Edward Maguire of the army engineers, and dated September 7, 1878. On the edge of this drawing is written in ink an unsigned statement that the cost of Fort Keogh up to September 17, 1878, had been:

Materials	$ 51,131.90
Transportation	74,192.81
Labor	57,975.72
	————————
	$183,300.43

On another edge of the plan in longhand—together with references to what apparently were inspection reports—is written a statement of buildings completed as of September 17, 1878. These were: commanding officer's quarters; fourteen sets of company officers' quarters (the drawing itself shows thirteen); three sets of infantry barracks, capacity three hundred men; one cavalry barrack, two hundred men; one granary, capacity seven hundred tons; quartermaster's storehouse; commissary storehouse; bakery; quartermaster's office; adjutant's office; and guardhouse. Buildings yet to be completed at that time, as recorded on the plan, were a hospital ("can be occupied now, will be completed in two months"), two cavalry barracks ("ready for use in a month or less"), twelve sets of officers' quarters ("ready for use in about three weeks"), four cavalry stables ("ready in ten days"), and a corral ("virtually finished").

In addition to the foregoing, the 1878 diagram of the fort shows the following contemplated buildings, some of which were never constructed: school teacher's house, post trader's buildings, sinks (latrines), bandmaster's quarters, ordnance officer's quarters, powder magazine, civilian employees' mess, blacksmith shop, post headquarters, regimental district headquarters, and a photographer's gallery.

Most western army posts were rectangular. Keogh was one of a few (Fort D. A. Russell, Wyoming, was another) built around a diamond-shaped parade ground. The commanding officer's quarters were at the west point of the diamond. Officers' quarters radiated in two directions from those of the commanding officer, and barracks for the men formed the other two sides of the diamond, converging at the east point. The cavalry stables were to the south of this point, and other buildings were scattered about the area.

Keogh looked somewhat un-fortlike. It was more like a small town.[6] The buildings were of wood, painted brown, with red shingle roofs. Officers' quarters were two-story duplexes and had dormer windows, small yards, and porches. There was no wall about the fort, though Miles for a time had long ricks of four-foot cordwood placed at strategic points where they might prove useful in the event of an attack, which never came.

Miles might have waited out the winter in his new base and begun his campaign in the spring. This was, in fact, what his superiors expected of him, especially in the light of General Crook's sad experience in winter fighting against the Sioux. Crook's command, called the Big Horn expedition, had, on

[6] Judy Nance, "Old Fort Keogh," manuscript, Casey E. Barthelmess Collection, Miles City (December 15, 1962).

March 17, 1876, on the Little Powder in Montana, attacked an Indian villege which Crook thought was Crazy Horse's. The village is still shown by that name in official records, although it was He Dog's village and Crazy Horse was not there. The immediate commander, Colonel J. J. Reynolds, Third Cavalry, had attacked in below-zero weather, driven the Indians from the camp, destroyed it, and captured their pony herd—but had lost it to the Indians when they rallied and counterattacked. That expedition had ended in near disaster for the troops (and in court-martial for Reynolds).

But this didn't deter Miles. He was, as he is said to have put it, "not the hiving kind," and the new base on the Yellowstone was not intended to serve as a hive. It was, in the Indian idiom of Mari Sandoz in her book *Crazy Horse* (p. 343), "like a wagon gun aimed against the heart of the people," the Sioux and their Cheyenne allies. Even before construction of the Tongue River cantonment was complete and before work on Fort Keogh had started, Miles was using the "bivouac" as a jumping off place to carry the fight to the Indians. The troops who began building the cantonment in August were engaging hostiles in October, skirmishing along the road from Tongue River to a supply camp downstream on the Yellowstone at the mouth of Glendive Creek, halfway to Fort Buford. Camp Glendive, as Miles called it, had been established before the Tongue River cantonment was set up, and served for a time as an intermediate point of supply for that post and Keogh, comprising, with Forts Keogh and Custer, the Yellowstone Command.

Colonel Miles himself, with a small escort, had a brush with hostile Sioux between Glendive and the Tongue River cantonment in early October, 1876, while reconnoitering the road to Fort Buford. A few days later, a wagon train of supplies for the Tongue River post was attacked by Sioux led by the Hunkpapa Chief Gall. The train turned back to Glendive for reinforcements, then made its way through to the Tongue.

Miles learned that the Indians causing this trouble were followers of Sitting Bull, who had slipped out of sight after the Custer battle. On October 17, Miles moved with the Fifth Infantry across the Yellowstone. He was in contact with the Sioux on the twenty-first, held two fruitless parleys with Sitting Bull in person, then attacked, driving the Indians from their camp and pursuing them for forty miles. At that point, two thousand of the hostiles quit fighting and gave five of their leaders as hostages to guarantee that the two thousand would go to their agencies and surrender, which they did. But Sitting Bull, Gall, and other leaders, with some four hundred followers, broke away and continued north through the snow and cold toward the Missouri. Miles returned to Tongue River Cantonment.

In his *Personal Recollections* (p. 218), Miles says that during that winter's campaign "all the mercurial thermometers we had with us were frozen solid." The cold was equal to that of Arctic regions. By the time they were outfitted for campaigning in temperatures fifty and sixty degrees below zero, his men looked like Eskimos. Beneath their woolen uniforms they wore underclothing made from woolen blankets. They had mittens and arctics, or buffalo overshoes, in addition to which they wrapped their feet in grain sacks. Most of the men wore crudely made buffalo-hide overcoats.[7] Woolen masks, slitted for their eyes, covered their heads. Officers had difficulty telling one man from another. These were infantrymen; in deep snow, they marched single file, the leader breaking the way as best he could and as long as he could, then retiring to the end of the column while the man next in line broke the snowy trail. They slept in the snow beside cottonwood fires. They crossed the Missouri, the Yellowstone, and the Tongue on the ice, with heavily loaded wagons and pieces of artillery. These operations continued from October until the middle of February.

So imbued was Miles—"Bear Coat," the Indians called him—with determination to carry out his winter offensive that he deplored the short stays his men had to make at the cantonment between their thrusts at the Indians. One reason for this was

[7] A large stock of these coats remained in storage after the fighting stopped. Sentries walking post in winter at latter-day Fort Keogh wore them. About 1896, the remaining buffalo coats were ordered destroyed, and they were burned by the wagonload. Some were not destroyed, however; Casey Barthelmess has two.

that a few traders and other civilians had moved in with the earliest troops and established near the fort a settlement that was christened Milestown, which later became Miles City. A major article of commerce there was liquor, which sometimes had a devastating effect on the troops. Miles, in his *Personal Recollections* (p. 232), asserts that several of his men dropped dead while making their wintry way between the traders' places and the bivouac.

Whatever some of his men may have done on post, in the field they were fighters. Following a brief respite after his destruction of Sitting Bull's camp in October, Miles was out again in December with four hundred infantrymen on Sitting Bull's trail. He divided his command into three columns, one of which, led by Captain Frank D. Baldwin of Michigan, on December 18 found Sitting Bull's new camp on the Red Water River, about forty miles west of Glendive. They attacked and captured the camp and some horses, although the wily old Sioux and his desperate little band again escaped.

Again Miles returned to Tongue River, again he reorganized to continue the winter campaign, and again he set out, late in December, in a foot of snow, this time to find the Oglala Crazy Horse, who was no more inclined to give up than was Sitting Bull. On January 8, 1877, at Wolf Mountain, near the Crook battlefield on the Rosebud, he found Crazy Horse's village and attacked, despite the fact that the Sioux outnumbered him two to one. In this battle Miles used artillery—two twelve-pound Napoleon guns, which he concealed under wagon covers on the march. When he unlimbered his "wagon guns" and began hurling shells at the Indians, they broke. It was not a bloody battle, despite the artillery, but it was decisive for it demoralized the hostiles and helped bring about the surrender at Fort Keogh in a few weeks of some three hundred of them, mostly Northern Cheyennes. Crazy Horse himself surrendered in May, at Fort Robinson, Nebraska, where four months later he was bayoneted to death while being put into the guardhouse.

Crazy Horse's defeat still left at large, besides Sitting Bull's small group, a camp of some sixty lodges of Sioux, principally Miniconjous, under Lame Deer. On May 2, 1877, Miles, with some of the recently surrendered hostiles as guides and scouts, set out from Tongue River to find Lame Deer's camp. This time Miles's command included four companies of the Second Cavalry, as well as two companies of the Fifth Infantry and four of the Twenty-second. His scouts found Lame Deer, on Muddy (now Lame Deer) Creek, near the Northern Cheyenne agency of today, which also bears the name of Lame Deer. The troops made a surprise attack at dawn, May 7, 1877. In the van, riding to help separate the surprised Indians from their horse herd, was Lieutenant Edward W. Casey, brevetted for his gallant service that day. The camp and horses were captured, fourteen Indians killed, and the remainder scattered—except for a small group including Lame Deer himself, who approached Miles as if to parley and abruptly fired at him. The shot missed Miles but killed a soldier behind him. In the ensuing turmoil, Lame Deer and his son were killed.

Some of Lame Deer's band stayed out several more months, as did Sitting Bull, who had meanwhile crossed the line into Canada, where he stayed four more years before returning and surrendering at Fort Buford. The Lame Deer affair was the last major encounter between the troops and the Indians in the war that had begun with an order for all hostiles to be on their reservations by January 31, 1876—the war that Washington said couldn't happen, the war that littered the plains with graves and brought about the belated building of Fort Keogh.

In the summer of 1877, although Fort Keogh was not yet finished and the troops were still quartered in the cantonment, the post was considered sufficiently habitable, in warm weather, for Colonel Miles's wife and daughter and his wife's sister to visit him there. The ladies enjoyed horseback riding, hunting, and boating on the Yellowstone; their presence, Miles said, "added a ray of sunshine to the life of the soldier." Families of other officers joined them the next year, when the better quarters at Fort Keogh were ready for occupancy. Arrival of the Fifth Infantry Regimental Band during the summer of 1877 also enlivened the social scene that ameliorated the harsh living and hard fighting that the forces stationed there endured.[8]

In 1877 an official inspection visit to the new fort was made by General of the Army William Tecumseh Sherman. This was the occasion for as much social to-do and as much military pomp and circumstance as could be mustered at a frontier post. General Sherman took advantage of the occasion to say that the "Sioux Indian problem, as a war question," had been solved by the new posts and by Miles's campaigns.

Lieutenant General Sheridan, commanding the Division of the Missouri, also inspected the Tongue River post and Fort Custer in the summer of 1877. In his report for that year, Sheridan said: "Both these posts are being pushed forward with the utmost vigor and will be of incalculable importance in closing up the troubles in the Sioux country."

But there was another war for Miles to help win for the army. This was the epic struggle by the Nez Percé Indians of Idaho to elude troops sent against them in 1877 as the result of continued friction between the Nez Percés and the settlers. The first army forces were soundly whipped, and then the Nez Percé Chief Joseph led his little band of rugged fighters on a masterly 1,200-mile flight by which he hoped to join Sitting Bull in Canada. The struggle spread over four months and three states, the Indians out-fighting and out-distancing the troops. On September 17, Colonel Miles was ordered out from Fort Keogh to intercept the Nez Percés. The Keogh expedition, four hundred men, including cavalry, artillery, and infantry mounted on captured Indian ponies, moved fifty-two miles toward the line of battle in twenty-four hours. In what Miles called "the crowning glory of our twelve days' forced marching," a surprise attack was mounted against the Nez Percés in the Bear Paw Mountains, northwestern Montana, on October 3. Casualties on the army side were heavy, and the Indian position proved so strong that Miles pulled back and laid siege to their stronghold. After three days, Joseph surrendered. Miles promised the Indians they would be returned to their Idaho homeland, but higher author-

[8] Miles, *Personal Recollections*, 256.

ities failed to support him and ordered the Nez Percés to Indian Territory, where illness and homesickness decimated them. Seven years passed before Miles succeeded in having those who survived sent back to Idaho.

Besides those recalled here, there were other battles, other heroes—red men and white—in the period that followed the building of the Cantonment on Tongue River. Miles and his men were only a part of it all; their part is emphasized here because of its association with Fort Keogh, which is the locale of this part of the Christian Barthelmess story. Many dramatic events took place at the fort. It was at Keogh (also at Fort Buford and Camp Poplar River) that remnants of Sitting Bull's band of Hunkpapas surrendered when they finally came back from Canada in 1881. At the cantonment in December, 1876, occurred what Miles in an official understatement called "an unfortunate affair": A little group of Oglalas led by their Sitting Bull (the "Good," he was called, to distinguish him from the Hunkpapa) rode in under a white flag to talk surrender terms for Crazy Horse, who apprehensively watched from a distance. Crow scouts for the army set upon the emissaries and killed most of them, including the Oglala Sitting Bull. This incident destroyed the peace move, and the war went on for another six months.[9] It was to Keogh that steamboats brought the soldiers wounded in the Nez Percé fighting, and, two years later, it was to the Keogh country that Little Wolf and Dull Knife—"Morning Star," his people, the Northern Cheyennes, called him—were allowed to return after their historic flight northward from exile in Indian Territory. Dull Knife died in 1883, in the Yellowstone valley, before his people had even been given a reservation of their own. Little Wolf lived out his unhappy days near Fort Keogh.

Today a stream of motor traffic ebbs and flows past the place where the old fort stood. The site is on U.S. Highways 10 and 12, which run through Miles City on Main Street and then southwestward to Billings and on to Yellowstone National Park. On the ground once occupied by Cantonment No. 1 stands the

[9] See Mari Sandoz on "The Lost Sitting Bull," in her book, *Hostiles and Friendlies*, 87.

Range Riders Museum, perpetuating in exhibits and photographs in Pioneer Memorial Hall the story of the soldier and the cattleman and other "Guardians of the Past," as a highway sign says at the museum turn-in. The sign is surmounted by a realistic life-size figure of a mounted cowboy, cut from sheet iron to a design drawn by Casey Barthelmess.

Fort Keogh's site is towards the west, across the highway from the Eastern Montana Fair Grounds. Since 1924 the few remaining buildings of the fort have housed the United States Livestock Experiment Station, maintained by the Department of Agriculture with the co-operation of Montana State College at Bozeman. In 1965 the superintendent of the experiment station was living in the house that was built for Colonel Miles, a stately twelve-room white frame structure topped by five red chimneys made of brick kilned on the site in 1877. A screened porch still shaded the front and one side of the house.

Modernity has erased many of the old landmarks at Miles City and the site of Fort Keogh. A police patrol radio tower stands now on Signal Butte. Neon lights along the motel-bordered highway make a little Broadway out of what not so long ago was a trail across sagebrush flats. The old days are gone, as irretrievably as are the dust devils that the wind sometimes picks up off the plains and sends whirling out of nothingness into nowhere. But still the Tongue flows down to the Yellowstone, and still the gray cliffs stand beyond the tree-lined streams, and still, for those who know what happened there, a haunting sense of history, like an evening haze, pervades the scene.

NINE

Gunnysacks Full of Old Papers

A DOZEN YEARS of soldiering in the Southwest lay behind Musician Christian Barthelmess when his regiment, the Twenty-second Infantry, was transferred in 1888 to Fort Keogh. That was the last year of Montana Territory; it became a state in 1889. By that time the Fort on Elk River, which was new in 1876, had played out its part in the "needless horrors of the Indian wars," and Nelson A. Miles had long since departed for new conquests in a career that eventually made him commander of the United States Army.

The telegraph came to Fort Keogh in 1878—soldiers on captured Indian ponies helped set up the lines. The telephone came a year later; the first line connected Miles's headquarters with the telegraph station. In 1881 the railroad arrived. The Northern Pacific built a station at the small town that had grown up near the post—so close the citizens could hear the bugles when the wind was right.

This settlement was first called Milestown, but when it was incorporated in 1887, it became a city. It had a school and churches, and everything else that went with such communities in those times, including saloons, dance halls (there were other names for them), real estate booms, newspapers, fraternal organizations, livery stables, and death and taxes—except that Milestown had no deaths in 1878 and only three births. As for taxes, the first assessment roll in 1877 for Custer County, of which Milestown was the seat, listed 113 taxpayers. The total levy that first year was $3,458.97, and $1,685.17 of this became delinquent.[1] The county, organized in 1877, was one of several

[1] W. E. Clarke, *Dusting Off the Old Ones*, 18.

Ice harvest on the Yellowstone.

The Sixth Cavalry's hunting expedition returns with venison for families on the post, December 1, 1904. Civilian teamster leaning on the wheel is Nelson; left foreground, 1st Sgt. Lawrence; the other three soldiers are Corp. Phillips, Sgt. McClusky, and Corp. Johnson.

These Fort Keogh officers are Capt. W. M. Whitman, Lt. W. E. Creary, Capt. C. W. Rowell, Capt. H. H. Benham, and Capt. Jacob H. Smith.

Christian Barthelmess identified this as "officers and ladies, also some Miles City people who came, saw, and were astonished" at some of the athletic and soldierly feats they witnessed at Keogh on a July the Fourth field day, probably 1905. Casey Barthelmess supplies these identifications: Capt. Van Patten Anderson seated center, his wife on his right; standing, Annia Ulio, third from left; then Mabel Towers, Lt. McCabe, Mrs. Ulio, Walter and Dr. Riggles; Mr. and Mrs. C. B. Towers on step; third from left, seated, wearing straw hat, Ruth Huffman, daughter of photographer L. A. Huffman. On left, front row, 1st Lt. A. J. Woude. Girl right front, with parasol, was daughter of Capt. Forsyth; she married Lt. McCabe.

Fort Keogh folks liked to square dance and often at a summer picnic improvised a dance floor by pegging canvas to the ground, as at this Twenty-second Infantry party. Right center, hand on hip, Musician Block; extreme right, Q. M. Sgt. and Mrs. Michael G. Giltinan; extreme left, their daughter, Genevieve.

The Reverend Isaac Newton Ritner, army chaplain at Keogh 1892–97, conducts a religious service. At the piano, Mrs. George Miles, the former Laura G. Ritner, daughter of the chaplain and wife of Nelson A. Miles' nephew, who was a paymaster clerk at Keogh. The Reverend Mr. Ritner was a Baptist who came to Keogh from Philadelphia.

The chaplain and the teacher go bird hunting. Mr. Ritner kneels left; daughter Laura holds the gun; white-haired woman, Mrs. Ritner. The vehicle in background is a Dougherty spring wagon, used by the army for transporting passengers. It was drawn by four mules, and had roll curtains and, in the rear, a "boot" or covered baggage rack.

Officers' wives occasionally visited them in their camps on practice marches. This is an unidentified group, early 1890's. The stove-equipped tent bears stenciled insignia of both the Twentieth and Twenty-second Infantry.

Faded though it is, this print from a Barthelmess negative of the early 1900's is reproduced for its historical value as evidence that women's life on an army post had its moments.

A buggy ride on a cold day could be something to do.

In the winter the parade ground in front of the commanding officer's residence was flooded, and the officers and their families went skating. Enlisted men had their rink elsewhere on the post. Background to this picture, headquarters building, band quarters (flagpole in front of it), guardhouse, and barracks.

Spectators at field day, 1905. Near buckboard, Col. Peter S. Bomus and Mrs. Bomus; driver, Tommy Thompson, son of H. C. Thompson and his Cheyenne wife. In second buckboard, Capt. Woude. The ambulance is driven by Fat Al Harding, civilian teamster, other occupants unidentified. In buggy at right, W. B. Jordan, early-day trader on Missouri River and at Fort Buford and Miles City ("he brought the first windmill into Montana"). Jordan's driver is Billy Smith, a stock detective. Post hospital in right background.—Identifications by Casey Barthelmess.

Capt. Charles L. Cooper, commanding A Troop, Tenth Cavalry, Colored, at Fort Keogh, about 1892. Lady unidentified. Cordwood pile stretches across the picture. Left, commissary sergeant's home. Background, Northern Pacific Railway tracks, and, beyond, the Camel Hump Hills.

Going into camp at McDowell's ranch, on the Tongue River
below Ashland, outer terminus of this particular practice march.

Water call at the McDowell camp.

The Miles City band came to the post to play for the July the Fourth program in 1904. Among its members were a number who had retired from the army and gone into business or taken jobs at Miles City. In front of bass drum, Morrison, conductor; right of drum, Al Furstnow, saddle shop; left, holding cornet, Tot Ruthier, then Barnholt, Carl Becraft, Joe Rusk (in derby), former quartermaster sergeant; Brandt, Ed Arnold (straw hat), Miles City merchant; Dr. Schrump, George Crowell, clarinets; Emil Knutson, horn; Frank (Stub) Taylor, who had a wooden leg and played a French horn in the band and a piano in downtown Miles City; Ernie Sorenson and Bill Theed, trombones; two unidentified; and, right end, George Crowell.

created out of the one named Big Horn, which, when it was organized in 1865, was called the largest county in the United States, comprising as it did the entire eastern part of Montana Territory from Wyoming to Canada.

From its beginning, Miles City was more than just an adjunct to the military post. It was an outfitting and supply base and transportation center for Black Hills mining operations, and a banking and trading hub for the cattle industry. Teddy Blue, in *We Pointed Them North* (p. 118) tells how it was: "Miles City was the cow town then [1883] for the north end of the range. The first Texas herds got up there in '80, and the Northern Pacific reached it in the fall of '81. There were plenty of places where Montana and Wyoming cattle could have been shipped, but Miles City had the best stockyards and, besides that, it appealed to Wyoming cowmen because they could follow the Tongue River in and have good grass and water all the way."

In a convention at Miles City in April, 1885, the Montana Stock Growers Association was created, through consolidation of two previously organized groups representing eastern and western parts of the territory. Written into the record as participants in organizing the early cattlemen are many names, including those of Granville Stuart, Conrad Kohrs, Pierre Wibaux, and a young easterner named Theodore Roosevelt then ranching just across the Dakota line.

Miles City has long since outgrown, though it still fondly recalls, its frontier cradle days. Today it is a lively little city with all the growing pains and other blessings of the age of speed and space. The 1960 census gave its population as 9,184, but in 1965 its Chamber of Commerce thought that 11,003 was a fairly accurate figure. Miles City has a State Industrial School, a country club, an airport, and a livestock saleyard. In its Range Riders Museum it preserves, along with countless other material reminders of its past, the epauleted full-dress uniform of Colonel Nelson A. Miles, his plumed hat and its carrying case, his saddlebags, and his ivory-handled revolver and holster. A city pumping station stands where in the old days the Yellowstone River steamboats docked.

When Fort Keogh was planned and built, in 1876–77, the studio, or gallery, for the post photographer was an eighteen-by-forty-foot, three-room, sod-roofed cabin made of cottonwood logs set on end and plastered with mud like the buildings at Tongue River Cantonment. The studio provided both working space and bachelor living quarters. Its first occupant appears to have been a photographer named John H. Fouch. Philetus W. Norris, second superintendent of Yellowstone National Park, writes of Fouch as being at the Tongue River Cantonment in the spring of 1877.[2] Fouch's signature appears on a letter of thanks from the passengers to the captain of the steamer *Josephine*. The letter was printed in the Bismarck (Dakota Territory) *Tribune* on June 8, 1877, along with information that the *Josephine* had departed Bismarck April 18 and reached Tongue River May 22. On November 13, 1878, the same paper reported that "John Fouch, photographer at Fort Keogh, passed east on Saturday" (November 11).[3]

The second tenant of the Fort Keogh studio seems to have been Stanley J. Morrow, of whom a good deal is told in *Frontier Photographer: Stanley J. Morrow's Dakota Years*, by Wesley R. Hurt and William E. Lass. Here it is well established that Morrow operated photographic galleries (contemporary sources say he "owned" them) at Forts Keogh and Custer from early autumn, 1878, until December, 1879. The third tenant was L. A. Huffman, who is quoted by Mark H. Brown and W. R. Felton in *The Frontier Years* (p. 34) as recalling that he arrived at Fort Keogh December 11, 1878.[4] Huffman, according to the same source (p. 42), remained there until about 1881, when he moved off the post to Miles City. He continued to live there for ten

[2] The Norris Papers are in the Huntington Library, San Marino, California.

[3] John S. Gray, "Photographic Strays and Mavericks," Manuscript, Chicago, 1964. Dr. Gray has found other evidence of Fouch's presence. See also his "Photos, Femurs and Fallacies," Parts I and II, *The Westerners Brand Book* (Chicago), Vol. XX, 6 and 7, August and September, 1964.

[4] Dr. Gray, in the manuscript previously referred to, questions Huffman's memory, saying that "Morrow was still flourishing at Fort Keogh in 1878," and adding that several details in Huffman's account of his own advent at Keogh are demonstrably erroneous. Dr. Gray concludes that it was 1879 when Huffman moved into the Keogh studio.

years, when he left for greener fields. He returned about 1898 to Miles City, and died in 1931 at Billings.

Soon after arriving at Fort Keogh, in 1888, Christian Barthelmess built his own studio with the help of other soldiers. It was a good-sized two-room structure made of rough lumber covered with tar paper and tin. His son Casey recalls that the north end of the larger room was covered with a canvas which could be used with a variety of settings as background for the taking of portraits. A clamp held the subject's head steady. There was a large skylight and there were four windows in the east wall. The studio housed two cameras, a large one for portraits and a smaller one for field work. There were corner shelves, closets, and a table, all filled with equipment and supplies. Part of the south end of the building was occupied by the dark room. Two large windows lighted the printing facilities; the rest of the room was storage space. The camera and a tripod for outdoor use were kept in a corner of this room. The studio was in the north part of the fort area, a quarter of a mile from the nearest of the main post buildings, in the section known as Soap Suds Row, which included the homes of married soldiers. Every western fort had a Soap Suds Row, so called because of the housewives and laundresses who lived in it.

A contemporary of Christian Barthelmess, Charles H. Watkins of Chicago, wrote Casey Barthelmess, in January, 1941, in part as follows:

> I was stationed at Fort Keogh when your father came there with the Twenty-second. I was a sergeant in H Company of the Fifth Infantry. I was a mounted messenger for the Quartermaster department at Keogh. Your father had quite a nice little photo gallery on the line where the enlisted men lived. I often went there to chat, because Thomas Kelly lived in the same row of houses, beyond the hay corral. His son John was post saddler, and a good friend of mine. I used Willis Rowland's horse to hunt with. Willis's little house and stable were just back of the hospital. My company of the Fifth built a bridge across the Tongue where it enters the Yellowstone. I used to watch your namesake, Lieutenant Casey, drill his Cheyenne scouts—what a time he had with them! Casey

had two large wolf hounds. His quarters were near the hospital. I spent five years in that country.

Casey Barthelmess has spent his life there. It was there he was born and grew into manhood, and it was near the old fort that he went back to live in his later years, near enough so that he can roam at will all the places he knew as a boy. It is all changed now, with government agricultural and livestock experts ensconced in such as remain of the old buildings that once housed the exciting busyness of an Indian-fighting army. Casey, treading his old haunts, conjures up many sights that no one else today can see, for once upon a time through a boy's eyes he looked upon the Indians, the soldiers, the bullwhackers, and the cowboys who are no longer there.

Casey's memories recall the bandstand in front of the commanding officer's quarters, the lofty flagpole on the parade ground, the cannon that was fired each evening at retreat—and always started a deaf dog barking. He remembers the honeywagon making its daily rounds to clean the latrines and collect the garbage. He sees Lieutenant McCabe sparking his girl in a fancy four-wheel buggy drawn by two white ponies hitched tandem, and sees, in the twilight, Larry Howe touching into brightness the kerosene lamps along the wooden sidewalks. He romps again in memory through the corrals and stables and shops and sheds, watches the Fourth of July field-day races, sees the summertime picnics along the river, with gay young couples dancing on canvas spread on the grass, or sees them in the winter skating on the flooded and frozen parade ground. The inviting odors of mess hall and supply room come back to him, as do the soft voices of the Cheyenne women who sometimes visited Mrs. Chris Barthelmess at the family home on the post. She would give them food and a round pan filled with water; they would eat, then wash their faces in the water and drink what was left in the pan, just as in recent years Casey has seen Indian women on the reservation do. While the women were visiting, the Cheyenne men, sometimes holding umbrella sunshades over their heads with one hand and the pony reins with the other, would ride about the fort and solemnly watch whatever there was to see. There was always something going on at the fort around the turn of the century, when Casey was a boy there, among the spruce young newly come shavetails and the dignified old campaigners who were still around, some of them bearing the scars of battle. Some of the old-timers stayed a long time.

"I can see them yet," says Casey, "gathered on a winter day toasting their shins, smoking and chewing, and spinning their yarns while they were sitting around the big old cast-iron stove in the blacksmith and wheelwright shop. That stove was really two stoves, for somebody—I think it was the old blacksmith, Hurley, and the wheelwright, George Cahoo—had taken a pair of army-issue box stoves and bound them together with iron rods and set them up on a brick hearth. This made an out-size stove that could be stoked with cordwood twice as long as the ordinary stove would hold. This saved a lot of sawing and gave more heat.

"George Cahoo was a pallbearer at my father's funeral. He married the widow Coonrad after Sergeant Coonrad was killed by road agents, in 1884, while on guard detail protecting the government pay roll for Fort Buford. That holdup and all the Injun fights and buffalo hunts that ever took place—yes, and some that didn't—were resurrected in the ruddy glow of that old double stove. I used to stand around and listen, too much, my mother thought. I remember hearing the old men talk about Yellowstone Kelly, the scout who as a young man, when he wanted to join up with Colonel Miles, scratched his own name on the paw of a bear he had killed and sent it to the Colonel in lieu of a calling card. He got the job and Miles rated him as a scout equal to Kit Carson or Daniel Boone. I remember a whiskered old codger who people told me was Johnson the liver-eater. He was a deputy sheriff at Coulson, later known as Billings, and he was town marshal at Red Lodge for a while, and occasionally came to Keogh.

"H. C. Thompson was a favorite of mine. He came to the fort in 1876 as first sergeant of E Company of the Fifth with Miles, and he lived until 1936. He was eighty-eight when he died.

He married a Cheyenne; they had a daughter and two sons. One of the boys was an athlete, used to pitch a lot of ball for the Miles City team. One time the wives of two soldiers got into a fight because one of them burnt her trash too close to the other woman's clothes hanging on a line. One woman threatened the other with a baseball bat, so, with the connivance of Lieutenant Foy, the officer of the day—who liked a good joke too—an off-duty private was enticed into walking post between their houses, carrying an outmoded rifle and a rusty bayonet, and that made both the women so mad they set out together to get Thompson, but he had disappeared.

"Then there was old Bill Rowland, 'last of the river trappers,' my father called him. He too married a Cheyenne and raised a family of boys. He and his son, Willis, who was a great friend of mine, were interpreters for the army, and worked with George Bird Grinnell when he was among the Northern Cheyennes writing books about them.

"And all those old Cheyenne warriors—the ones who fought their way back to Montana from Indian Territory in '78 and all the rest of them—I can never forget their wrinkled old faces, with sorrow and dignity and patience written on them like lines on a battle map! I saw and knew, in my boyhood, Two Moon, who fought Crook at the Rosebud, Custer at the Little Big Horn, and Mackenzie at Dull Knife's village, and surrendered to Miles at Fort Keogh in 1877. He lived a long time—long enough to go to New York in 1913, with other old chiefs, to help President Taft break ground for a national Indian memorial at Fort Wadsworth, a memorial that was never built—another unkept promise to the Indians. Two Moon was practically blind then, and had to be led. He said he didn't know how old he was.

"I remember Wolf Voice, who was a Casey scout. Remember what Frederic Remington wrote about Wolf Voice? Said he had 'a grand face, tremendous physique, and enough self-containment for a High-Church bishop.' I knew Yellow Robe, who was the last of the Cheyenne scouts to die. He passed away in 1957 in the Veterans Hospital at Miles City. In his last few days, he wouldn't open his eyes or take a drink of water. He finally managed to tell me through an interpreter—Little Wolf, grandson of the famous old Cheyenne chief—what he hadn't been able to make the nurses understand—that the light from the windows hurt his eyes and he couldn't drink water through a glass tube. So the nurses pulled down the blind and gave him water in a cup.

"Clearest of all, I remember Little Chief of the Cheyennes. He died in 1906, when I was sixteen. I had great admiration for him, as did my father, who knew him intimately. I think the picture my father took of Little Chief at Fort Keogh in 1892 just about tells, in that old Indian's face, the whole tragedy of his people."

Casey's friendship with the Northern Cheyennes brought him in 1959, at the Miles City Diamond Jubilee, a distinction of which he is proud—that of being adopted into the tribe and given the name of Howling Wolf, which had belonged to one of the old-timers in the days when the fighting Cheyennes were making their last stand in the Powder River country.

Sometimes, to help bring into sharper focus his memories and his knowledge of events that occurred at Keogh before his own time there, Casey Barthelmess leafs again through a sheaf of old army papers pertaining to Fort Keogh which were found some years ago in the attic of the old commissary building on the post. They were stuffed into two gunnysacks. The man who found them gave them to Casey.

The earliest of the papers (they are no longer in gunnysacks) is a letter dated September 1, 1876, signed by Captain Charles McClure, chief, Commissary of Subsistence, Headquarters Department of Dakota, St. Paul, Minnesota. Directed to "A.C.S. [Assistant Commissary of Subsistence], Post on Tongue River, M.T., via Fort Buford," this letter transmits a printed circular of information on how to operate a patent no-keyhole combination bank-lock on an iron safe shipped to Tongue River August 4 from Chicago. An invoice dated July 7, 1877, covers four half-chests and two quarter-chests of tea. There is a request, July 12, 1877, that to a previous request for rations for General Miles' command there be added "600 rations of each of the component parts of the ration and 120 cans of corned beef, 340 cans of tomatoes, 48 cans of salmon and 100 boxes of sardines for the use of the officers." There are invoices for eight cases (four hundred pounds) of Vanity Fair tobacco, and quantities of soap, candles, hard bread, potatoes, onions (2,900 pounds in one order, December 30, 1876), sugar, coffee (sacked), allspice, cinimond and codence [sic], milk, raisins, granulated eggs, vanilla extract, prunes, beans (baked), and blacking (shoe). The troops ate lots of meat. Dated November 1, 1876, at Tongue River, is an order signed by First Lieutenant Frank D. Baldwin, Fifth Infantry, for ten thousand rations of beef on the hoof to be provided, with two herders, "for the expedition about to leave this cantonment."

An 1879 receipt for thirty-two head of beef cattle for the Second Cavalry shows that the bunch weighed 25,600 pounds or a net average of 800 pounds and that the price paid was five and one-half cents a pound. These were heavier than a herd of two hundred head, concerning which Colonel John Gibbon, commanding the District of Montana, wrote to Fort Keogh on June 12, 1877, from Fort Shaw. Gibbon's letter informed the commander at Keogh that R. S. Tingley had contracted to deliver the two hundred, averaging 600 pounds each, "at the mouth of the Tongue about July first."

Fresh beef, flour, beans, coffee, sugar, vinegar, candles, soap, salt, and pepper constituted the rations for "a citizen severely wounded by Indians and admitted to Post Hospital," according to Voucher 16, Abstract of Provisions, in June, 1877, signed by Second Lieutenant Charles F. Roe, Second Cavalry. Lieutenant H. K. Bailey, Fifth Infantry, signed a Ration Return for bacon, coffee, and sugar for his company (twenty-eight men) for ten days, the issue being "to replace rations lost on a night march, March 25, 1879." Much of the paper work dealt with loss or damage incurred in transportation of supplies. "By command of Brigadier General Terry" on August 22, 1877, Captain R. P. Hughes, Third Infantry, addressed to Department Headquarters at St. Paul a communication which sounded off as follows concerning a Board of Inquiry: "Why were the stores invoiced to Tongue River not delivered there? Were they all detained at Fort Buford? By what authority did the steamboats unload at Fort Buford? Did no one receipt to the steamboats for the stores landed at Fort Buford? If anyone receipted to the steamboats he must know what he receipted for. The stores did exist at one time and it is not shown by these proceedings that the Board has exhausted its power in getting information as to what became of them."

A requisition for subsistence stores for Fort Keogh from June 1, 1880, to June 30, 1881, gave the following "Strength, Estimated," for that period:

Fifth Infantry, ten companies	450
Battalion Second Cavalry, four cos.	300
Laundresses	20
Matrons	2
General staff	4
Enlisted Indians	70
	——
Total	846
Civilian employees	100
Visiting Indians	50

Among the old papers in the gunnysacks, Casey Barthelmess found three bearing his father's signature. One related to commutation of rations while on furlough in August, 1892, for the sum of $10.75. The others were small printed forms on which soldiers certified that articles purchased by them at the post commissary were for their own use. These show that Barthelmess on one occasion in 1891 bought miscellaneous supplies including "1 lb. Tobacco, Dur.," and five pounds of "apples, Evap'd," and that on another date the same year he signed for "1 spool Thread, Linen, Black."

"Rock Road—His Mark" is the signature for one dollar's worth of sugar and coffee bought by one of Lieutenant E. W. Casey's Cheyenne scouts. Other Indian names appearing on the documents include those of Two Moon, Walks Night, Bob-tailed Horse, Braided Hair, and Poor Elk, as well as Little Chief, who in May, 1892, drew rations at Keogh for "a party of ten for five days while visiting at the post."

And so they run—yellowed pages of the record itself, full of the little matters of which great events are compounded—messages of all shapes and sizes, on many kinds of paper, fragile now with the erosion of time and the dreamless dust. Some have been charred on their edges by fire, many show water stains, and the ink on most is faded. They date from the earliest days of the Tongue River Cantonment; all except those subsequent to 1890 are in longhand. They deal not with battle orders but with such affairs as the transfer of men from one duty to another, rations or clothing issues, canteen requisitions, reports on lost shipments, and investigations of damaged goods. Quantities involved range from beef on-the-hoof to a plug of tobacco. Many proud old army names appear on these antique scraps of paper— Terry, Gibbon, Miles, Whistler, Baldwin, Randall, Swaine, Roe, Ord, and Ulio. Some are written in a script that struts across the mildewed pages with ruffles and flourishes; some are plain, firm, strong. All of them say something, to the sentient eye, about the men who, leaving these perishable papers behind them, inscribed their names on the indestructible pages of history.

---··{ TEN }··---

Shadow Catcher Loses a Friend

WHEN forty-three-year-old George Washington reined his horse under an elm on Cambridge Common, July 3, 1775, drew his sword, and took command of the heterogeneous forces comprising the first army of the thirteen American colonies, its ragged ranks included a company of Stockbridge Indians from Massachusetts, "in feathers, paint and nakedness." From the early settlement period along the Atlantic seaboard and the Spanish *entrada* in the Southwest, Indians served often and effectively as allies of the invading conquerors of their race. Both as scouts and as regular soldiers on both sides in the Civil War, Indians fought so well that when Congress in 1866 enacted legislation reorganizing the federal armed forces for postwar purposes, it authorized the enlistment of one thousand Indian scouts on the western frontier.[1]

Military leaders on the plains and in the deserts and mountains learned early in the game that sometimes only an Indian could catch an Indian. Crook and Miles used Apache against Apache in Arizona and New Mexico in the 1870's and 1880's. At the Rosebud, in Montana in 1876, Crow and Shoshoni scouts rode with the troops. Wearing tribal garb and flaunting "a barbaric pride of arms," they so impressed a newspaperman accompanying the expedition (he was not fond of Indians in general) that he wrote: "I felt a respect for the American Indian that day."[2] In the same year, 350 Pawnee, Shoshoni, Arapaho, Sioux, and Cheyenne scouts rode with Mackenzie against Dull Knife's village in the Powder River country. Miles compli-

[1] Ganoe, *History of the United States Army*, 3, 307.
[2] John F. Finerty, *War-Path and Bivouac*, 117.

---··{ 99 }··---

mented the "loyalty and courage" of his Cheyenne and Sioux scouts when he captured the Nez Percés in 1877, although later he expressed a lack of confidence in a few of his Apache scouts—and replaced them with other Apaches. General Eugene A. Carr had some of Frank and Luther North's Pawnee scouts with the Fifth Cavalry at the battle of Summit Springs in 1869, but he never cared much for them. In 1876, however, when preparing for his part in the Big Horn and Yellowstone expedition, he asked for Pawnee scouts, but higher authorities denied his request. On New Year's Day, 1891, while serving with the Sixth Cavalry in the Wounded Knee campaign in South Dakota, John J. Pershing, then a second lieutenant, commanded a unit of Sioux scouts in action against their hostile tribesmen. The official record of the event shows four killed—all on the hostile side. This skirmish provided the first combat citation on Pershing's record. Years later he wrote that he had "found much that was fine in Indian character."[3] His chief scout was a Sioux named Bear Nose, who to his last years enjoyed boasting, "Me heap scout, General Pershing, all right, all right!"[4] Paiutes, Seminoles, Navahos, Arikaras, Osages, Delawares, and men of other tribes at many times and places helped the army win the Indian wars.

Once in a while the Indian aides let the army down. Three Apache scouts—Sergeant Dead Shot, Sergeant Dandy Jim, and Corporal Skippy—were hanged at Fort Grant, Arizona, March 3, 1882, after a court-martial found them guilty of mutiny, murder, and desertion. These three and some others "hitherto of unblemished character for fidelity" became so excited by the incantations of an Apache medicine man, Nock-ay-del-klinne (the name is variously spelled), whom they were supposedly helping to arrest because he was inciting war, that they fired on the troops when fighting began. This was on Cibicu Creek, near Fort Apache, Arizona, August 30, 1881.[5]

Such perfidy was rare. And even after most of the fighting in the West was over, the army remained committed to the use

---

[3] Richard O'Connor, *Black Jack Pershing*, 34.

[4] Lewis A. Lincoln, manuscript, Denver, Colorado, 1964.

[5] Carter, *Yorktown to Santiago*, 228.

of Indian scouts in patrolling the border as it was slowly tamed down. Secretary of War Redfield Proctor, in his *Annual Report* for 1891–92, summed up the general experience by saying that the conduct of Indian scouts and police employed in military and quasi-military duties had been so satisfactory that each of the twenty-six regiments then serving west of the Mississippi was authorized to enlist one company of Indians. The Secretary had inspected Indian troops, and he commended their good conduct, military bearing, and care of their arms, equipment, and quarters. He warned, however, that great care should be taken in the selection of officers for duty with Indians. Such officers should be men of high character who believed in the work and in the possibility of progress and civilization for the Indian, men patient and faithful, "imbued with the missionary spirit."

Perhaps he was thinking then of men like First Lieutenant Edward Wanton Casey, Twenty-second Infantry—Ned to his fellow officers, Big Red Nose to the Indians. Certainly Casey met Secretary Proctor's specifications, for it was he who led into action in 1890–91 a mounted troop of Northern Cheyenne scouts who had everything—*élan, esprit de corps*, regulation equipment down to white dress gloves, and even their own printed stationery—

Troop L, 8th Cavalry
"Casey's Scouts"
Fort Keogh, Mont.

—and stood up well under fire.

Lieutenant Casey's roots were in New England. The family homestead was a farmhouse built about 1750 on Boston Neck, a narrow bit of land bordering on Narragansett Bay near Wickford, in the southeastern part of Rhode Island—"Little Rhody," smallest of the states, historically important for Roger Williams and an early struggle for freedom from tyranny. The Lieutenant's father, Silas Casey, was born there, was graduated from West Point in 1826, was brevetted a major in the Mexican War, and a major general for distinguished service in the Civil War. General Casey is remembered, in addition to his combat record, for compiling in 1862 a three-volume revision of Hardee's *Rifle and Light Infantry Tactics*, which had been published in 1855. The revision, entitled *Infantry Tactics*, was almost universally known as "Casey's *Tactics*" and became the most widely used manual for Civil War purposes. Volunteer officers found it invaluable in turning recruits into disciplined fighting men. General Casey died in 1882.[6]

One of the General's sons, Thomas Lincoln Casey, stood first in the West Point graduating class of 1852, was brevetted for Civil War service, and in 1888 was appointed chief of the Corps of Army Engineers (retired 1895, died 1896). Another son of General Silas Casey, named after his father, was graduated from the United States Naval Academy in 1860. He rose to the rank of rear admiral, retired September 11, 1903, and died August 14, 1913, at Warm Springs, Virginia. One daughter of the General married Brigadier General Lewis Cass Hunt of Wisconsin, who left a long record of meritorious Civil War soldiering. Another daughter married Colonel Robert Nicholson Scott, United States Army.[7]

The son who became Lieutenant Edward Wanton Casey was born December 1, 1850, on the far side of the country from the New England homestead—at Benicia Barracks, near San Pablo Bay, north of San Francisco, while his father was in California as a captain in the Second Infantry. At the age of nineteen Edward Casey followed the family footsteps to West Point, graduating thirty-fourth in the class of 1873. Soon after being posted to the Twenty-second Infantry at Fort Sully, Dakota Territory, he volunteered for duty with Custer's Black Hills expedition of 1874, but his application was not granted. He served through civil disturbances at New Orleans in 1874, returned north with his regiment the next year and participated in the 1876 campaign against the Sioux and Cheyennes.

In the autumn of 1876, Casey's regiment and the Fifth Infan-

[6] Heitman, *Historical Register of the U.S. Army, 1789–1903*, I, 289; Ganoe, *History of the United States Army*, 285.

[7] Heitman, *Historical Register of the U.S. Army, 1789–1903*, I, 289; *Stockgrowers Journal*, Miles City, Montana, January 10, 1891; Joseph M. O'Donnell, archivist, West Point.

try regiment were stationed on the Yellowstone, the Fifth at Cantonment No. 1, Tongue River, the Twenty-second at the mouth of Glendive Creek. Late in the fall, Casey and his command went to Cantonment No. 1 with the Fifth. There are papers extant which bear Casey's signature as post adjutant at Tongue River in November, 1876. Here Colonel Miles placed Lieutenant Casey in command of a company of scouts composed of white citizens and Indian guides. They were in the affair at Wolf Mountain, January 8, 1877, and in the attack May 7 on Lame Deer's village on Muddy Creek by the Second Cavalry and the Fifth and Twenty-second Infantry, where the action occurred that won Casey a brevet for gallant service.

In the same year, a small detachment led on a patrol by Lieutenant Casey reached a point where it became necessary to cross the swift Tongue River, swollen by heavy rains to such an extent that some of the men faltered. Casey plunged in and set the example that such a crisis called for. Thereafter his men called him Tongue River Casey.[8]

For the next few years, Casey's service was varied. It included strike duty in the East, at Chicago and at Wilkes-Barre, Pennsylvania, garrison duty at Fort Brady, Michigan, and more Indian campaigning, in 1879 and 1880, in Texas, Indian Territory, and Colorado. On August 28, 1880, he became an assistant instructor of tactics at West Point. For four years he held this position, which must have provided special interest because of his father's contribution to the literature on infantry tactics. In 1884 the Lieutenant rejoined the Twenty-second at Fort Lewis, Colorado. It was during this tour of duty that he led the military reconnaissance to the Grand Canyon, described earlier. For this purpose, in 1887, he resigned the regimental adjutant's duties that had been assigned to him on September 1, 1884. In June, 1888, the Twenty-second, still under command of Colonel Peter T. Swaine, was ordered to replace the Fifth Infantry as the gar-

---

[8] *Twenty-second Annual Reunion of the Association of the Graduates of the United States Military Academy at West Point, New York, June 12th, 1891* (Saginaw, Mich., 1891). (Obituary of Edward W. Casey, No. 2501. Class of 1873. 47–49.)

rison at Fort Keogh, Montana. Here Casey's leadership qualities came to full flower.

At an officers' school at Fort Keogh in the winter of 1889, he read a paper on the subject of training Indians as soldiers. Colonel Swaine decided to have Casey organize a troop of scouts to be recruited from the Indians of the area, the Northern Cheyennes. Civilian opposition had to be overcome in order to achieve the thoroughness that Casey desired. The commissioner of Indian affairs thought military service was incompatible with progress in "civilizing" Indians. Casey presented his views in writing, and was authorized to go ahead.[9]

Cheyennes had served individually with various army units as scouts in the closing phases of the war of 1876–77. Two Moon, White Bull, Brave Wolf, and other warriors, after surrendering to their erstwhile foes, threw in with them and helped bring in the reluctant hostiles. At that time these scouts were not subject to military training and discipline; but Casey enlisted his scouts as regulars and trained them to live, drill, and fight as soldiers subject to the same discipline as other troops. He brought his unit to a knife-edge sharpness that helped cut down the Sioux "uprising" of 1890.

Casey's scouts were paid twenty-five dollars a month, and were supplied with issue uniforms and equipment. They were enlisted for six months at a time, but were subject to discharge when the need for their services no longer existed "or at the discretion of the commanding officer." They were honed to a professional sharpness that won the admiration, among others, of Frederic Remington, who was at Fort Keogh in the summer of 1890. He had accompanied an Indian commission on a tour of the Northwest, and later that year rode with Casey's scouts during their participation in action at Pine Ridge. Remington was there as artist-correspondent for *Harper's Weekly*. Two of his articles, "Lieutenant Casey's Last Scout" and "The Sioux Outbreak in South Dakota," were included in 1895 in his first book, *Pony Tracks*. Of Casey as a soldier Remington wrote:

[9] *Stockgrowers Journal*, January 10, 1891, quoting "an officer of his own regiment."

Ridge Walker, who is said to have gone to see Wovoka, the
Ghost Dance prophet. He died an old and highly respected man.

Plenty Horses, Sioux Indian who killed Lt. Casey, January 7, 1891, on the Pine Ridge Reservation in South Dakota.

Red Tomahawk, one of the Standing Rock police who killed Sitting Bull on December 19, 1890. Casey Barthelmess does not know when or where his father took this photograph or the one of Plenty Horses; after his father's death, they were found in his studio.

White Moon, Cheyenne Indian scout who was with Casey when the Lieutenant was killed.

Spotted Hawk.

White Bull, who served with Miles in 1877 and later enlisted in
Casey's scouts. He was a medicine man and, after the Northern
Cheyenne reservation was established in 1884, became one of
the tribal judges.

Fire Wolf, shown behind the Barthelmess studio, Fort Keogh. In background is Soap Suds Row, Barthelmess home at right.

Eddie Gray, Northern Cheyenne, who died in 1960, aged 82. He was a good friend of the Barthelmesses. This photograph has been reproduced elsewhere (Mark H. Brown and W. R. Felton *The Frontier Years*, 194) as "A Cheyenne Warrior, with war drum." The object he holds is a shield. Barthelmess took the photograph in his Fort Keogh studio about 1891.

Hairy Hand, one of the scouts, with his wife, who holds a framed portrait of their dead child.

Little Eagle,
sometime after
1892.

Bird Wild Hog, whose father was one of the headmen under Little Wolf and Dull Knife. Bird Wild
Hog was noted among the Cheyennes as a particularly fine dancer, much admired by women. At
the time of his discharge from Casey's scouts, on
May 15, 1891, at Fort Keogh, his age was given as
22 years. He died in 1940. Christian Barthelmess
called him Hedge Hog.

Christian Barthelmess identified this boy as the son of Scalp
Cane, one of Casey's scouts. The lad holds a wooden flute.

Bright Eyes, they called her.

His name was Dives Backward.

Tall Girl.

Little Chief, head of a band of Cheyennes who lived for years with the Sioux at Pine Ridge, S.D., before settling down on the Cheyenne reservation at Lame Deer. Another pose has been erroneously identified as Little Wolf (Martin F. Schmitt and Dee Brown *Fighting Indians of the West*, 39). The crosslike ornament on Little Chief's breast is an emblem of the four directions. It is made of thin German silver plate brought to the Cheyennes by traders. Nelson A. Miles was fond of old Little Chief, who in his last years was never happier than when he was listening to an army band.

"The sun will never shine upon a better." And he thus described his first sight of Casey's scouts "on a cool morning at Keogh" (pp. 5, 38): "Patter, patter, patter—clank, clank, clank; up comes the company of Cheyenne scouts who are to escort the general—fine-looking, tall young men, with long hair, and mounted on small Indian ponies. They were dressed and accoutred as United States soldiers, and they fill the eye of a military man until nothing is lacking."

Another friend of Casey's was in the area at this time: George Bird Grinnell—naturalist, ethnologist, writer-editor. In his writings Grinnell refers in two places to the Lieutenant. In the preface of *The Cheyenne Indians*, he says: "My first meeting with the Cheyennes was hostile,[10] and after that, though often in the country of the Cheyennes, I never knew them until their wars were over. My first visit to their camp was in 1890 when, at the invitation of my old schoolmate and friend, Lieut. E. W. Casey, 22d Infantry, who had enlisted a troop of Cheyenne scouts, I visited him at Fort Keogh and made their acquaintance . . . . From that time on, no year passed without my seeing the Cheyennes." In *The Fighting Cheyennes*, Grinnell again recalls the episode, but remarks that when he reached Fort Keogh, Casey was in the mountains getting out timber, so he missed the lieutenant, "but I saw his scouts and was interested in the promise they gave of making an excellent body of soldiers" (p. 434).

One reason for Casey's success in handling his troop lay in the fact that he had good clay to work with. Once a woodland tribe, the Cheyennes came westward long ago, and early in the eighteenth century they were living in earth lodges and growing crops as did other sedentary tribes—Mandan, Hidatsa, Arikara— on the upper Missouri. Then the Cheyennes acquired the horse

---

[10] In 1870, Grinnell made his first trip west, as a member of a paleontological expedition led by Professor O. C. Marsh of Yale University. The party was occasionally threatened by remnants of Tall Bull's Cheyenne band which had been attacked the year before at Summit Springs by General Carr and the Fifth Cavalry. Grinnell wrote about the Pawnees and Blackfeet in 1889 and 1892. The depth and dedication of his scholarship are indicated by the fact that only when he had studied the Cheyennes for twenty-five years did he begin writing about them, and then he said he was "constantly impressed by the number of things about the Indians that I do not know."

and became nomadic buffalo hunters on the Northern Plains. Bent's Fort on the Arkansas River in Colorado, which was built about 1833, was a favorite trading post for the roving Cheyennes, some of whom remained in that area and became the Southern branch of the tribe.

From the time of their earliest contacts with white people, the Northern Cheyennes were distinguished for their courage and pride of bearing, their quick and strong intelligence, and their tribal pride. Captain William Philo Clark, of the Second Cavalry, White Hat to the Cheyennes, whom he befriended and whose final surrender he helped accomplish to the end that the killing might stop, said of them in a book on the Indian sign language that he published in 1885:

> The men of the Cheyenne Indians rank as high in the scale of honesty, energy, and tenacity of purpose as those of any other tribe I have ever met, and in physique and intellect they are superior to most tribes and the equal of any. Under the most demoralizing and trying circumstances they have preserved in a remarkable degree that part of their moral code which relates to chastity, and public sentiment has been so strong in them in regard to this matter that they have been, and are still, noted among all the tribes which surround them for the virtue of their women.[11]

The National Archives has found among its old army records a muster-roll for Casey's scouts for the month of June, 1891, by which time Lieutenant Casey was in his grave and the troop's day in the sun was fading. But his Cheyenne soldiers were still known by his name, for the muster-roll so designated them. The unit was still L Troop, Eighth Cavalry; its commander then was First Lieutenant Robert J. Duff, functioning in the absence of Captain Edward Edgar Wood who was on teaching duty at West Point.

The muster-roll bears the comment by Lieutenant Duff that this was the first roll of the troop since December, 1890. Fourteen Indians were on this roll; all were privates and had enlisted

[11] Clark, *Sign Language*, quoted by James Mooney, "The Ghost-Dance Religion," *Fourteenth Annual Report of the Bureau of American Ethnology*, 1027.

(in some cases re-enlisted) during June, 1891, at Fort Keogh, for a period of five years. These men were:

Arapahoe Chief	Spotted Elk
Bear Tusk	Standing Elk (Arthur)
Bites	Standing Elk (Eugene)
Mexican Cheyenne	Sweet Grass
Red Antelope	Tall Bull
Rock Road	Walks Fanning
Round Stone	Wooden Leg

Two others were shown attached to the troop: Wolf Voice, a corporal, enlisted September 6, 1890, at Fort Keogh, and Big Leg, a private, enlisted January 22, 1891, at Pine Ridge, South Dakota. The last two, according to "Remarks" on the muster-roll, were "entitled to forty cents a day for use of horse and equipments."

At the Northern Cheyenne Agency, Lame Deer, Montana, there is no official list of Casey's scouts, but two older members of the tribe have put down on paper the names of those whom they remember as having been in the troop. Casey Barthelmess obtained one such list from John Stands-in-Timber, who was born on the reservation in 1884. Stands-in-Timber went to school at Carlisle and at Haskell. He was one of the tribal patriarchs and in 1965 was still living in the log house that had been his and his wife's home for forty years. He is generally considered to be the tribal historian. His list of Cheyennes who were, at one time or another, in the scout troop, carries sixty-six names. A list was also given a few years ago to the Reverend Father Peter J. Powell of Chicago, an adopted member of the tribe, by Rufus Wallowing, son of one of the scouts and a resident on the reservation. The Wallowing list bears fifty-one names, of whom thirty are categorized as "Old Scouts," that is, men who first enlisted for service under Miles in 1877 and in 1889–90 comprised the nucleus of L Troop as organized by Lieutenant Casey. Others who joined in 1890 are said by Wallowing to have come largely from Little Chief's band of Cheyennes, who lived for

some ten years at Pine Ridge with the Oglala Sioux, returning in
1890 to Tongue River.

Here is Rufus Wallowing's list of Old Scouts:

Beaver Heart	Old Bear
Black Crane	Ridge Bear
Black Stone	Rising Sun (Philip)
Bobtailed Horse	Rowland, Willis (mixed
Braided Locks	blood)
Brave Wolf	Shell
Buffalo Wallowing	Stump Horn (Frank)
Bull Sheep or Ram	Sun Bear
Clubfoot (John)	Tall Bull (Jacob)
Dog (Louis)	Two Moon
Elk River or White Elk	Weasel Bear
Hairy Hand	White Bull
High Walker	White Shield
His Bad Horse	White Wolf
Little Sun (Charles)	Wolf Name
Man Bear	

Other names on one or both of these lists include:

American Horse	Kingfisher
Big Bat	Little Bear
Big Head	Little Bird
Big Nose	Little Eagle
Black George	Little Head
Black Horse	Little Whirlwind
Black Medicine	Lone Elk (Charles)
Black Wolf	Low Wolf
Chubby	Medicine Bear
Crane	Medicine Bull
Crazy Dog	Pine (Frank)
Crazy Mule	Red Bird
Eagle Feathers (John)	Red Fox
Eyes Yellow	Red Man
Flying	Red Robe
Grasshopper	Ridge Walker (Robert)
Hollow Breast	Short Tree
Kills Night	Rowland (Zachary)

Seminole (Miles) White Bird
Shavehead White Moon
Sponge Wild Hog
Starving Bear Wolf Voice
Strange Owl (John) Woman Leggings
Teeth (Charles) Wounded Eye
Turkey Legs Yellow Fox (Robert)
Twin Yellow Man
Wesley Merritt[12] Yellow Robe

Among these men with the odd names were many individuals bearing traits that are universally valued, men with personalities widely differing from one another and widely differing from a stereotyped concept of the Indian. There was, for instance, Elk River (*Mo-a-yo-ha*). His name, which was also borne by a member of the Southern Cheyenne tribe, was the Cheyenne name for the Yellowstone. For years Elk River was a familiar and respected figure around Fort Keogh. One of his daughters married H. C. Thompson, Fifth Infantry sergeant and later Fort Keogh civilian wagon master.

Early in life Elk River rejected certain Cheyenne traditions and rituals. In one reversal from custom, he shunned aggressive warfare. According to Grinnell (*The Cheyenne Indians*, II, 3): "He just lived his life, took care of his family, and held the respect of the whole tribe. He was a most generous man, and at the same time a man with a remarkable sense of justice. He was a skillful catcher of wild horses, and it is said that on several occasions he rode up beside a wild horse and put a hackamore on it before stopping it." Elk River was in Dull Knife's village when it was destroyed by Mackenzie in 1876; Grinnell says (*The Fighting Cheyennes*, 365): "Elk River, more thoughtful of his family than of fighting, cut a long slit in the back of his lodge with his knife, and drove out the women and the little ones, helped them to cover, and then returned to try to save the horses."

John Stands-in-Timber in August, 1962, told Father Peter

---

[12] This was a Cheyenne named Scabby Horse; translation difficulties put him into the records under the name of the distinguished brigadier general.

Powell: "Elk River, Sun Road, Porcupine, and Day Man all enlisted in Indian Territory. When they came up here to Montana they enlisted again. Elk River used to tell us how they chased horses down Horse Creek, where the plains tribes signed the treaty, below Casper. Along that creek and back to the mountains, they chased horses. They ran down colts, catching them before their mothers got back. Sometimes they would use a loop of rawhide. More often they caught colts on foot. Elk River was the first [Cheyenne] man to wear coat and pants all the time. He wore pants with a yellow stripe down them. His mother, Short Woman, who was real old, used to call me nephew. Elk River was old when he enlisted in the scouts, and was said to be nearly a hundred when he died, about 1908." Many variations appear in estimates of Elk River's age. He first enlisted as a scout in 1879, in Montana, under Miles, after which he went to Indian Territory. He re-enlisted on returning north. His service in the army indicates he was not a complete pacifist, and Stands-in-Timber also recalls hearing Elk River sing and seeing him dance in ceremonies recounting Cheyenne war victories.

The book *Horse Catcher* by Mari Sandoz is based upon the lives of this man and his counterpart among the Southern Cheyennes. The book is dedicated "To the two great Cheyennes named Elk River, both council chiefs and peace men, one the keeper of the sacred arrows of the Cheyenne Indians, the other the greatest horse catcher of all the High Plains."

The Wild Hog on the list of Casey's scouts was Bird Wild Hog, whose father was one of the headmen under Little Wolf and Dull Knife, leaders of the Northern Cheyenne break from Indian Territory in 1879. Mari Sandoz says (*Cheyenne Autumn*, xv) that the senior Wild Hog was "a big broad man with a broad humorous face," and that the son was nicknamed Little or Young Hog. Christian Barthelmess, in identifying a photograph he took of the son, wrote the name as "Hetch [Hedge] Hog." Casey Barthelmess remembers him as an unusually expert dancer, much admired by women. His discharge, dated at Fort Keogh May 15, 1891, said he was born in Wyoming, was twenty-

two years old, six feet tall, copper complexion, black hair and
eyes, and by occupation when enlisted (September 18, 1890) a
hunter. Bird Wild Hog died August 31, 1940. His widow Lydia,
daughter of old Little Wolf, was killed at Sheridan, Wyoming,
in 1958—when she was ninety—by an automobile.

White Bull was one of the Northern Cheyennes who surrendered to Miles at Fort Keogh in 1877. He was held by Miles
as a hostage for the surrender of others, and a few days later
he was the first of thirty Cheyennes recruited by Miles for scout
duty. He was in the group on Muddy Creek when Lame Deer
tried to kill Miles. White Bull scalped Lame Deer and his
nephew, who were both killed by soldiers at that time. Miles in
his *Recollections* credits White Bull with saying that when he
settled down on the reservation, he wished to have a garden in
which he could grow raisins. In his late years he was still an
important personage among the Cheyennes, as indicated by
the fact that Christian Barthelmess, in identifying the photograph he took of this old warrior, wrote his name: "Jutch [Judge]
White Bull."

Grinnell (*The Fighting Cheyennes*, 287) says that White Bull,
who was a medicine man, made the war bonnet that Roman
Nose (Bat) wore when he was killed with the Cheyennes fighting against the army scouts at Beecher Island in 1868. It was an
exceptionally fine bonnet and would protect its wearer against
death so long as certain taboos were observed. One taboo was
that the wearer should eat no food that had been touched by an
iron fork. The night before the Beecher Island fight, Bat un-
knowingly violated the taboo. This broke the medicine that protected him. The medicine could have been renewed by pre-
scribed ceremony, but there was no time for this. So Bat went
into the Beecher Island fight knowing he would be killed.
He was.

Ridge Walker, one of Casey's scouts, is remembered by Casey
Barthelmess as a Cheyenne of high intelligence. Grinnell speaks
of him (*The Cheyenne Indians*, II, 250) as "notable for his industry and his success in cultivating the ground." Ridge Walker
was the son of Beaver Claws, and was one of three Northern

Cheyennes who, when the Messiah or Ghost Dance movement was in its infancy, made a pilgrimage to Nevada to learn of the doctrine from its originator, the prophet Wovoka. He promised return of the good old days of unspoiled freedom for the Indians. The two who went to see him with Ridge Walker in the autumn of 1890 were Porcupine (whose report to his tribesmen on his return kept him talking for five days) and Big Beaver.[13] Other Cheyennes later made the same pilgrimage, and the Cheyennes accepted the doctrine, but to a lesser extent than did the Sioux. The Messiah fervor induced no outbreak, nor serious threat of one, among the Cheyennes. In his later years Ridge Walker was herder of a bunch of beef cattle that the government for a time maintained on the Northern Cheyenne reservation to feed the Indians. John Stands-in-Timber says Ridge Walker's helpers were Willis Rowland and Prairie Bear. Beef from the herd was issued to the Indians up until about 1910. Ridge Walker's widow, almost ninety, was still living in 1965.

Wovoka, the Indian messiah whom Ridge Walker and others went to see, was a Paiute sheepherder, given the name Jack Wilson by the non-Indian rancher who adopted him and brought him up under Christian influences in a home near Walker Lake, Nevada. Wovoka, after a couple of years in California, Oregon, and Washington, returned to his people in the late 1880's, when he was about thirty-five, and became a shaman, or medicine man. Influenced by the Shaker religion, to which he had been exposed in the Northwest, despondent over the passing of the old, and bewildered by the coming of the new, Wovoka in 1889 began telling of visions in which God came to him and promised a rebirth of freedom.

Wovoka's message, imparted to other tribes through their emissaries to him, was that the time was at hand for reuniting the Indian people, living and dead, on a regenerated earth, to live a life of aboriginal happiness, free from disease, hunger, misery, and death. Wovoka urged the Indians to make them-

---

[13] "Report of an Indian Visit to Jack Wilson, the Payute Messiah," by Albert S. Gatschet, in *The Journal of American Folk-Lore*, Vol. VI, No. 21 (April–June, 1893), 108–111.

selves worthy of the new day by discarding warlike things. They should practice generosity, honesty, and good will. In its beginning, the teaching was of peace, but as it spread among other tribes, and as they began ghost dancing to hasten the coming, excitement and hysteria were generated. Especially was this true among the Sioux of the Dakotas, acutely suffering from "an accumulation of miseries,"[14] including insufficient food and clothing. Night and day beating of the dance drums panicked the settlers in the Indian country. Newspaper scareheads increased the excitement. Civilian authorities, unable to cope with the situation, turned to the military, and an ugly little war ensued, centering on the Pine Ridge Reservation of the Oglala Sioux in south-central South Dakota. Nelson A. Miles, by that time a major general commanding the Division of the Missouri, directed the campaign. It brought into the field about 5,500 troops, almost half the infantry and cavalry strength of the army at that time.[15] The first troops on the ground, November 20, 1890, were the Ninth Cavalry and the Eighth Infantry from Fort Robinson, Nebraska, and the Second Infantry from Omaha. They moved swiftly on the reservation; reinforcements followed, including the Seventh Cavalry from Fort Riley, Kansas, the Sixth Cavalry from New Mexico and Arizona—and, from Fort Keogh, Casey's scouts.

Christian Barthelmess, Lieutenant Casey's friend and admirer from the time they got lost together trying to find the Grand Canyon—the time a soldier fell down a well at Cortez—photographed the scouts when they were just organizing, on through their period of training, and now as they went to war—as well as on their sorrowful return some weeks later. When the troop was first organized, the scouts and their families were housed in tipis and tents, in a camp on the Yellowstone one and one-half miles upstream from Fort Keogh. Casey, even while he drilled the Indians, put them to work, with the help of soldiers, cutting logs, rafting them down the river, and building

[14] Mooney, "The Ghost-Dance Religion," 826. In his section on "Causes of the Outbreak," Mooney cites a number of authoritative statements showing that the Sioux had suffered as the result of "unfulfilled promises" by the government.
[15] Robert M. Utley, *The Last Days of the Sioux Nation*, 251.

their own cantonment. This work was still in progress when the trouble broke out at Pine Ridge and Casey's scouts dropped their construction work to go to war.

The scouts trotted out of Fort Keogh on December 7, 1890, and marched to Belle Fourche, South Dakota, nearly two hundred miles southeast. There they entrained on the Chicago and Northwestern Railroad, which took them and their horses via Rapid City to Hermosa. Thence they marched again, to the Pine Ridge area, where, on December 24, 1890, they joined the command of Lieutenant Colonel George B. Sanford, Ninth Cavalry, camped on the left bank of White River opposite the mouth of White Clay Creek. The main camp of the hostiles was near the home of an Indian named No Water, on White Clay about eight miles from its mouth. In the hope of preventing a major clash between the Sioux and the army, now glaring down gun barrels at each other for the first time since 1876, the troops sought to maintain surveillance over the camp, figuratively showing the Indians simultaneously an open hand and a clenched fist. There were skirmishes with small bands of warriors seeking to break through the cordon. In these patrols, Casey's scouts acquitted themselves well under fire. Meanwhile the Sioux were still ghost dancing, particularly a large band of fanatical warriors who had isolated themselves in a stronghold position on Cuny Table, a mesa in the badlands north of Pine Ridge.

Sitting Bull, in his camp on Grand River in South Dakota, forty miles south of the Standing Rock Agency at Fort Yates, North Dakota, came under suspicion as an inciter. His arrest was ordered. At dawn on December 19, Indian police sought to make the arrest. Sitting Bull, his son, and eight others of his band were killed, along with six Indian police. The same day, a ragged band of Miniconjou Sioux, led by Big Foot (also called Spotted Elk), set out from their reservation, Cheyenne River, South Dakota, moving southwestward with a vague objective that eventually found them headed for Pine Ridge, to the accompaniment of much activity by troops trying to intercept them.

The interception was finally accomplished, and the Seventh

Cavalry under Colonel James W. Forsyth was sent in to disarm them at their surrounded camp on a creek called Wounded Knee. On the morning of December 29, when the disarming began, fighting broke out, and before the Seventh's carbines, revolvers, and artillery—four automatic Hotchkiss guns firing two-pound explosive shells—finally fell silent, 25 soldiers and 128 Indian men, women, and children lay dead on the wintry plain. Thirty-five officers and men and 33 Indians were wounded.[16] Whose was the right and whose the wrong is still debated; one historian's conclusion, that it was "a regrettable, tragic accident of war," is perhaps as good as any.[17]

The Pine Ridge Agency was fortified, and there was a small fight at a near-by mission, for armed Indians in considerable numbers were moving about within the wall of surrounding troops. Casey's scouts performed "outstanding service" in this situation. As the tension eased, some of the Cheyennes were in almost daily contact with Sioux on a friendly basis. On January 6, 1891, several of the hostiles visited Lieutenant Casey in his camp. Their attitude led Casey to believe he might help bring about a peaceful finale to the painful affair if he could talk personally with some of the Sioux leaders.

There was precedent for this belief. In Arizona, in 1886, the Apache chief, Geronimo, and his band of elusive hostiles had been talked into surrendering by First Lieutenant Charles B. Gatewood of the Sixth Cavalry, who at the risk of his life rode into the Apache camp, accompanied only by a few friendly Apaches, and demanded that the hostiles lay down their arms and come in, which they did. Carter, historian of the Sixth Cavalry, in recounting this incident, calls it "an act which made him [Gatewood] known throughout the army and the country generally, and which Ned Casey probably had in mind" five years later at Pine Ridge.[18] And Robert N. Getty, first lieutenant and

[16] *Chronological List of Actions*, Adjutant General's Office, 55.
[17] Utley, *The Last Days of the Sioux Nation*, 230.
[18] Carter, *Yorktown to Santiago*, 251–52, 268. Tragedy ended Gatewood's army career, as it did Casey's. Gatewood in 1892 was with a Sixth Cavalry squadron sent from Fort McKinney, Wyoming, to the JA Ranch on Crazy Woman Creek to prevent bloodshed between the invaders and the so-called rustlers in the Johnson County cattle war. The troops arrested fifty of the in-

regimental quartermaster, Twenty-second Infantry, second in command of Casey's scouts, in an official report to the Assistant Adjutant General, Department of Dakota, written April 13, 1891, at Fort Keogh, said: "I now think that Lieut. Casey started out with the intention of penetrating the hostile camp to have a talk with the principal chief, and thought he could accomplish his object by boldness."[19]

It was January 7, 1891. Lieutenant Casey rode out in the morning from his White River camp toward the main camp of the Sioux, who had rallied around Red Cloud and other "still arrant chiefs," upstream on White Clay Creek, where the surrounded Indians were thinking things over, almost, but not quite convinced of the futility of further resistance.

Six men were present at the tragedy that ensued. Five who lived to tell about it included the following men:

Plenty Horses (*Tashunka-ota*), a Brulé Sioux, who had survived Wounded Knee. His life had been shaped in part by his attendance at the Carlisle Indian School in Pennsylvania.

Broken Arm, a Sioux whose home was on Medicine Root Creek, and who happened to be with Plenty Horses.

Bear Lying Down, another Sioux, from the hostile camp, identified in contemporary newspaper dispatches as an uncle of Plenty Horses.

Pete Richards, a Sioux mixed-blood, married to a daughter of Red Cloud. Pete was one of many descendants of John Richards (sometimes spelled Reshaw), a "fiery little Frenchman" who in the 1840's had become a whisky trader among the Sioux and had sired a "clan of joyous warriors, scouts, interpreters and traders."[20]

White Moon, one of Casey's scouts, who rode out with him that morning. Christian Barthelmess, in identifying a photo-

---

vaders and took them to Fort McKinney. The building in which they were held caught fire; the blaze threatened the post. Working with a backfire, Gatewood was crippled by a powder explosion. He retired from the army and died a few years later.

[19] Secretary of War, *Annual Report, 1891,* 281–82.

[20] George E. Hyde, *Red Cloud's Folk: A History of the Oglala Sioux Indians,* 52–53, 94–96.

graph he took of White Moon, wrote on it that as a result of this day's deeds the Indian tried to kill himself.

As usual in cases of sudden crime, stories of the witnesses differed in details, but a distillation of the official reports shows in the main what happened. Lieutenant Casey, riding toward the Sioux camp, came upon a group of Indians. He stopped to chat. At this point, one of Casey's Scouts named Rock Road, who had started out from the army camp with Casey and White Moon, decided to go no farther, turned his horse, and rode back to camp. Casey, White Moon riding behind him, went on. About one and one-half miles from the Indian camp they encountered Bear Lying Down. Casey asked him to go back to the Sioux camp and tell Red Cloud or other chiefs to come out and talk with Casey. Bear Lying Down did as the Lieutenant asked. But Red Cloud did not choose to go talk with Casey; instead, he told Bear Lying Down to return to the Lieutenant, tell him that Red Cloud was planning to go to Pine Ridge the next day for a talk with army officers, and that meanwhile Lieutenant Casey should go away at once because his life was in danger so near the hostile camp. Red Cloud told Pete Richards to go with Bear Lying Down.

Riding out to deliver Red Cloud's message, the two came upon Lieutenant Casey and White Moon, talking with Broken Arm and Plenty Horses, who had come riding by. They were "close to an old stable," Casey a little distance from the others. The Lieutenant shook hands with Richards, who delivered Red Cloud's message. All six men were now close together. Broken Arm asked Casey if he could go back to the army camp with him to look for some missing horses; Casey replied, "All right." His horse and Richards' were facing each other, and each man turned his mount, to go his separate way.

Plenty Horses, who had backed his own horse into a position behind Casey, lifted his Winchester rifle and fired one shot into the back of the officer's head.

Bear Lying Down had started away. At the sound of the shot, he wheeled his horse in time to see Lieutenant Casey fall to the ground dead. Plenty Horses, rifle on his arm, rode toward the

Indian camp. Broken Arm dismounted, took Lieutenant Casey's cartridge belt and two revolvers from his body, and handed them to White Moon. Another Indian, named No Neck, rode up; he urged White Moon to take all the Lieutenant's belongings back to the army camp, but White Moon declined to touch anything other than the revolvers, although he did lead back the slain officer's horse. After telling Bear Lying Down to get word to Red Cloud, Richards followed White Moon and they went together to the headquarters of Brigadier General John R. Brooke, in command of the troops along White River.

There the two told of the shooting. Richards said he did not see Plenty Horses fire, but when he turned at the sound of the shot, he saw the rifle still at Plenty Horses' shoulder. Lieutenant Getty, who had been Casey's aide in training the scouts, assumed command on his death and led a detachment of the troop to the scene of the shooting and brought in the body. First Lieutenant B. L. Ten Eyck, assistant surgeon, examined it and wrote in his report that "the bullet entered about at the occipital protuberance median line and emerged below the right orbit. No other wounds or injuries." This tends to offset the statement by a Cheyenne scout named Wooden Leg who (in his autobiography, as interpreted by Thomas B. Marquis) says, "The Sioux scalped Big Red Nose and took all his clothing." It also contradicts testimony given at the subsequent trial of Plenty Horses to the effect that an Indian cut off one of Casey's fingers to steal his cameo ring.

However, Casey Barthelmess remembers hearing H. C. Thompson say, years later at Fort Keogh, that one night at Pine Ridge soon after the killing, a Sioux Indian appeared at Lieutenant Getty's tent in the army camp and showed what he said were Casey's gold teeth, dislodged by the bullet that killed him. The Indian said he had found the teeth on the ground near the body, and wanted money for them. Lieutenant Getty opened the door of his Sibley stove and threw the teeth in the fire.

The night of the shooting, Lieutenant Casey's body was taken by wagon to the town of Oelrichs, South Dakota, and placed in charge of the army quartermaster. The next morning, accompanied by a noncommissioned officer, the corpse was started on the journey to Boston Neck, Rhode Island, where it was buried in the family cemetery, a walled tract in a pasture on the Casey homestead. Captain Thomas L. Casey, then on duty in New York, and other members of the family met the train. The monument over the grave is inscribed:

Edward Wanton Casey
Son of
Gen. Silas and Abby Perry Casey.
1st Lieut., 22nd U.S. Infantry.
Born December 1, 1850.
Killed January 7, 1891,
While reconnoitering a camp of
Hostile Sioux Indians.
"One of the most brilliant
and beloved officers of the service."

The quotation is from General Miles' official report to the Adjutant General of the Army, dated January 7, 1891.

Casey's murder was an act that made sense to no one except perhaps the youth who fired the shot. Plenty Horses was arrested in February, indicted for murder by a federal grand jury at Deadwood in March, and tried at Sioux Falls in April. The jury disagreed. Another trial was held in May, and this time Plenty Horses was set free on a directed verdict by the court, which ruled that the killing was committed by a combatant during a state of war and hence was not a criminal act. Plenty Horses' motivation he himself explained at his trial: "I am an Indian. Five years ago I attended Carlisle and was educated in the ways of the white man. I was lonely. I shot the lieutenant so I might make a place for myself among my people. I shall be hung and the Indians will bury me as a warrior. They will be proud of me. I am satisfied."[21]

[21] Utley, *The Last Days of the Sioux Nation*, 266. The year that Plenty Horses killed Casey, Frank E. Lewis, a teacher in No. 2 district, Pine Ridge, was killed from ambush by Eagle Horse, a young Sioux afflicted with tuberculosis, who explained that knowing he was dying he killed the white man so he might have

About a week after the Casey affair the capitulation of the Pine Ridge hostiles was completed, and on January 21, 1891, the military forces that had been set in motion by a Paiute sheepherder's dream marched in grand review before General Miles and his staff and then returned to their stations. The Ghost Dance War was over. There was little in it for anyone to be proud of, aside from individual instances of courage in line of duty. The Indians slain at Wounded Knee were buried in a common grave on the hill where the Hotchkiss guns had stood. The dead soldiers were dealt with slightly better. Their government spent ten dollars apiece for coffins and offered free transportation to the nearest national cemetery. Any other arrangement was at the expense of family or friends.

Leading the riderless horse of their fallen chief, Casey's scouts, Lieutenant Getty commanding, rode back into Fort Keogh from Pine Ridge on a January day of 1891 in a blizzard with the temperature at thirty-five degrees below zero. Christian Barthelmess' camera recorded the return, in a photograph that froze the scene in all its frosty pathos.

Later on, when Lieutenant Casey's estate was settled, his horse—the one he rode the day he was killed, a spirited, well-bred black, Casey's personal property—was purchased by Colonel Swaine, commander of the Twenty-second Infantry and of Fort Keogh and Lieutenant Casey's superior officer since the Fort Lewis days. Colonel Swaine in 1894, the year before he retired from the army, shipped the horse from Fort Keogh to a California ranch which he had acquired in anticipation of retirement. The ranch was at Los Nietos, now a part of the city of Los Angeles. Colonel Swaine detailed Musician Christian Barthelmess to accompany the horse on the journey and make sure the animal had good care. As a compliment to Colonel Swaine, the Northern Pacific Railway transported the horse and its caretaker without cost. This was in return for services rendered early in 1894 when Colonel Swaine was stationed at St. Paul, Minnesota, February 5 to May 15, as commander of the Department

company on his journey. (*Fifty-ninth Annual Report of the Commissioner of Indian Affairs, 1890*, 54.)

Christian Barthelmess called this "the start of Casey's scouts."
Lt. Casey sits on log in center. Standing from left, Bull Sheep,
Zachary Rowland, Hollow Wood, Sweet Medicine, unidentified
Indian. On Lt. Casey's left stands "Old Bill" Rowland, whom
Barthelmess called "the last of the old-time river trappers." Row-
land was also an interpreter, and aided George Bird Grinnell in
his research among the Cheyennes. Indians seated right include
Hairy Hand and Wolf Name. Photograph taken in 1889 at the
scouts' camp on the Yellowstone, west of Fort Keogh.

The scouts in column, Casey center, Getty left. Army reports of the period said these and other Indians showed "remarkable aptitude for military service, were amenable to discipline, generally of good habits, proud of their occupation."

Top center, Wooden Leg, one of the scouts, at the last minute
decided he did not want his shadow caught in the white man's
box, and turned his back, about 1890.

From left, standing: Bird Wild Hog; Willis Rowland and his Cheyenne wife; Ridge Walker with an eagle feather in his hat; and H. C. Thompson and his wife, also a Cheyenne. Girl in front of Ridge Walker is Nancy Big Hawk, who married Rufus Dives Backward. On the horse, with rifle in hand and pistol in belt, the Thompson son, Tommy.

Elk River, one of Casey's scouts, and his wife, the parents of
Mrs. H. C. Thompson. Elk River preferred hunting wild horses
to waging war. Mari Sandoz' book *Horse Catcher* is in part based
on his life.

The room at Fort Keogh occupied by 1st Lt. Francis C. Marshall when he was in command of Casey's scouts, 1892–93, following Lt. Casey's death. On the wall, a ghost shirt, which the Sioux in the Ghost Dance War thought would turn the soldiers' bullets. Wounded Knee proved otherwise.

Miss Sophia Swaine, at the family home in Los Nietos, Calif., in 1897, with Lt. Casey's black horse, which Col. Swaine had purchased from Lt. Casey's estate and shipped to the Swaine home by train and boat, in charge of Sgt. Chris Barthelmess.

Scouts with women and children: Rock Road stands high on left,
Willis Rowland on right. Mrs. Rock Road, wearing a plaid shawl,
stands center; left, Mrs. H. C. Thompson; Mrs. Stump Horn, in
broad-striped black and white blanket. Seated in front with
child in arms, Mrs. Wolf Name.

Mrs. Otis Fingers, Mrs. Strange Owl, and Mrs. Chasing Bear, jerking meat. It was cut in strips and hung on racks to weather and become dried beef. Near Lame Deer, about 1891.

Always there were Indians around Fort Keogh, whose site had long been a favorite Cheyenne camping ground. Barthelmess wrote on this picture (1889): "Wolf Voice and family except one which is mine [Leo, aged three]." Left, Wolf Voice, a Northern Cheyenne army scout who at this time was an agency policeman. Right, Yellow Robe (he and Wolf Voice married sisters), who died in 1959, the last survivor of the Cheyenne scouts.

Barthelmess dated this Northern Cheyenne camp scene 1890. Bark on cottonwood trees has been chopped off for firewood. Over the tipi door is a medicine bundle, tentatively identified by Father Peter J. Powell as the *Hohk tsim*, a sacred wheel-lance of the Cheyennes. Protruding from the bundle is the carved end of the lance, representing the face of Sweet Medicine, Cheyenne culture hero.

Stump Horn's tipi in winter camp near Fort Keogh, 1890.

Some of the Indians in this winter camp near Fort Keogh enjoyed the luxury of wall tents, perhaps even stoves inside the canvas walls, about 1889.

Stump Horn, one of the scouts, and his family, with children inside the protective cage on the travois or pony drag. One of several Barthelmess photographs of the Stump Horns, this picture was taken near the scout camp at Fort Keogh in 1889.

Cheyenne camp, 1890, near Fort Keogh. Foreground, a sweat
lodge. For ceremonial purification rites, the willow framework
was tightly blanketed, water was poured on heated stones inside
the lodge, and the resulting steam bath cleansed body and spirit.
From camps such as this came Casey's scouts.

Two of the "Rowland boys," James and William, with their Indian families. The men were sons of William (Old Bill) Rowland and his Cheyenne wife. The Rowlands were highly respected by red men and white.

of Dakota. During that period, Jacob S. Coxey's army of the unemployed marched on Washington (April 29). Colonel Swaine directed the military protection of railroads and other utilities in Minnesota, Dakota, Montana, Wyoming, and Idaho during the migration of twenty thousand unemployed.

On the journey to California, Musician Barthelmess scarcely let the horse out of his sight. From Fort Keogh to Portland, Oregon, the horse's baggage car was shared by the man, who had a cot in the corner. From Portland the trip was made by steamship to San Pedro, California, near Los Angeles. At the Los Nietos ranch, Barthelmess photographed Miss Catherine Sophia Swaine, daughter of Colonel and Mrs. Swaine, on the porch of the family bungalow, with the horse in the driveway. Lieutenant Casey had been among the admirers of the colonel's daughter.[22]

Colonel Swaine retired January 21, 1895. He was succeeded in command at Fort Keogh by Colonel James Seaman Casey of Pennsylvania, a distinguished soldier who had been brevetted for services in the Civil War and brevetted and awarded the Medal of Honor for gallantry January 8, 1877, in Miles's attack on Crazy Horse's village at Wolf Mountain, Montana. (The Colonel and Lieutenant Casey were not related.)

Casey's scouts, in the few remaining years of their existence, were commanded by Lieutenant Getty, who became a captain in the Twenty-second Infantry in 1896, transferred in 1899 to the First Infantry, and in 1901 rose to the rank of major; and by Captain E. E. Wood and First Lieutenant Robert J. Duff, both previously mentioned, and First Lieutenants Francis C. Marshall, Eighth Cavalry, Henry Clay Hodges, Jr., Twenty-second Infantry, and William David McAnaney, Eighth Cavalry.

For a fleeting period, the record set by Casey's scouts helped stimulate the army's recruitment of Indian units for scouting and for regular duty. Infantry companies were organized and placed under non-Indian officers. One company of Oglala Sioux was built to full strength at Pine Ridge and stationed for a time

[22] Casey Barthelmess recalls hearing his mother tell of his father's trip with the horse, and his recollections are verified in the manuscript (referred to in note 3, Chapter Six) "Memoirs of My Father and Mother," by Colonel Swaine's son, Charles.

at Fort Omaha, Nebraska. Company I, Sixteenth Infantry, at Fort Douglas, Utah, was made up of Brulé Sioux—Plenty Horses' people. Apaches recruited at the Carlisle Indian School and at San Carlos, Arizona, formed an infantry company at Mount Vernon Barracks, Alabama.[23]

But the sun was setting on the day of segregated Indian soldiers. There was little field duty now for the army, and garrison routine was dull business for young men brought up in the tradition that war is a natural state. Some, as their enlistments expired, enrolled in agency police squads. Adaptation to reservation life steadily thinned the ranks of Indian troops.

Casey's scouts passed into history on May 4, 1895, when Colonel Casey reported to the Adjutant General, Department of Dakota: "In compliance with Department Special Orders No. 64, the twenty-seven enlisted men of Troop L, Eighth Cavalry, were this day discharged from the service of the United States."

So it was elsewhere as the frontier closed and the West filled up and settled down. In September of 1891, the total number of Indians in the army, scouts and regulars, had been 837, but by 1896 it was 131. On May 31, 1897, fifty-three Indians comprising Troop L, Seventh Cavalry, were discharged and a last lingering unit came to an end.[24]

A brief resurgence of need for Indian scouts occurred as late as 1916. That was the year when President Woodrow Wilson sent General Pershing into Mexico to get Francisco ("Pancho") Villa, a revolutionary who, in March, 1916, led a raid on Columbus, New Mexico, in which sixteen Americans were killed. The Eleventh Cavalry, a unit in Pershing's punitive expedition, with a company of twenty-five Apache scouts in the van, surprised and routed a Mexican force on May 5 at Ojos Azules, killing some forty of the enemy. First Lieutenant James A. Shannon commanded the scouts. A fellow officer, writing of this engagement, reported: "As First Sergeant Chicken of the Apache scouts said, when asked for his opinion, 'Huli! Damn fine fight!'"[25]

[23] Secretary of War, *Annual Report, 1892*, 49, 94, 123.
[24] Secretary of War, *Annual Report, 1892*, 196–97, and *Annual Report, 1897*, 218.
[25] First Lieutenant S. M. Williams, Eleventh Cavalry, in *U.S. Cavalry Journal,*

That was the last time that Indians enlisted as Indians fought for the United States. But when World War I came, eight thousand American Indians, three-fourths of them volunteers, joined the armed forces. This was a factor in the passage in 1924 of a Congressional act that gave all Indians citizenship. In World War II, twenty-five thousand of them, men and women, served— not in separate units but in the ranks as equals of the best.[26] Tongue River Casey would have liked that.

January, 1917, quoted in Colonel Frank Tompkins, *Chasing Villa*, 194. A *New York Times* dispatch from Columbus, New Mexico, April 6, 1916, reported that these scouts were recruited at Fort Apache, Arizona, by Captain Oliver Perry Morton ("Hap") Hazzard, Tenth Cavalry. The *Times* dispatch gave Sergeant Chicken's Apache name as *Eskenahdesta*.

[26] U.S. Department of the Interior, Office of Indian Affairs, Chicago, 1945, *Indians in the War*, 1. Awards won in World War II by American Indians included seventy-one Air Medals, fifty-one Silver Stars, forty-seven Bronze Star Medals, thirty-four Distinguished Flying Crosses, and two Medals of Honor.

ELEVEN

Taps Along Tongue River

ISCHARGED at Fort Keogh on December 1, 1891, Musician Christian Barthelmess re-enlisted on December 2. Five years later, that period of service ended, but the next day he was back in the army again for his fifth enlistment. He was transferred in 1896 from the Twenty-second Infantry to the regimental band of the Second, which had replaced the Twenty-second as the Fort Keogh garrison. For the rest of his time in the army, the Second was Barthelmess' regiment.

It was a changing army in which he served during that last decade of the nineteenth century. In 1891 the system of geographical military divisions was discontinued; commanders now reported directly to the General of the Army, at Washington. Troops were better fed, housed, and equipped—the Krag-Jörgensen repeating rifle and carbine replaced the Springfield. The men were kept busy, not by long night journeys through the snow to burn an Indian village, but by routine drill, practice marches, and camps of instruction in field maneuvers. The army was, as usual, below authorized strength, but even so it was becoming more selective in its recruiting; 74 per cent of the 26,174 applicants for enlistment in 1891 were rejected as unfit. The percentage of foreign-born recruits was still high—about half. Desertions, which had plagued the army in the Indian war days, numbered in 1891 only 1,503, which was 841 fewer than the year before and 1,332 fewer than in 1889. The policy now was to abandon the smaller and more isolated forts and concentrate troops at larger posts, near civilian centers of transportation and communication. By the end of 1891, twenty-eight posts, one-fourth the number occupied in 1889, had been abandoned, and a dozen more were about to be closed. Fort Keogh, with a garrison of two cavalry troops and eight infantry companies, was one of those kept.[1]

One reason for this was that Keogh was only eighty miles from Lame Deer, the agency for the reservation on the Tongue River where the Northern Cheyennes were groping their way along the first hard uphill stretches of the white man's road. They had a late start—which helps explain why they have in some respects made slower progress toward economic self-sufficiency than some tribes have done. Too, the fighting in the late 1870's killed off many of their potential leaders. Other Montana Indians had been established on reservations years before the Northern Cheyennes had any land of their own to live upon following their surrender. The Southern Cheyennes acquired their reservation in Indian Territory in 1867, although they didn't settle down on it till 1875. After the close of the war period, many of the Northern Cheyennes lived with the Sioux on the Pine Ridge Reservation in South Dakota. Others camped around Fort Robinson, Nebraska, and Fort Keogh, along the Yellowstone, the Tongue, and the Rosebud—homeless in their homeland.

Not until November 26, 1884, were the Northern Cheyennes finally assigned to a reservation of their own. This was done by an executive order, signed by President Chester A. Arthur, giving the tribe 271,000 acres east of and adjoining the Crow reservation on the Little Big Horn.[2] White settlers occupied parts of the tillable areas along the streams when the land was assigned to the Cheyennes; twenty years passed before Congress finally bought the white people out and they moved away.

The Northern Cheyennes in their early reservation years underwent a period of heartbreak, but they were used to that. In their wars with the army, and especially in their Homeric struggle homeward from Indian Territory in 1878–79, they suffered heartbreak that only a strong people could have survived. The Cheyennes' strength lay in self-confidence based upon a

[1] Secretary of War, *Annual Report*, 1891, 4, 16, 52, 55, 63.
[2] Frederick Webb Hodge, *Handbook of American Indians North of Mexico*, II, 378.

primitive social structure that had given them not only the courage to defend their way of life but a way of life that was worth defending. They lost the struggle, but they retained their tough resilience as a people who refused to be crushed out. In surviving they had little help from the government that had beaten them down.

The first school for the Northern Cheyennes was provided not by the government but by four nuns from the Ursuline Convent at Toledo, Ohio, who responded to the call of Bishop Brondel of the Diocese of Montana for volunteers to go into the wilderness as missionaries to the Cheyennes. The four nuns—Mother Amadeus and Sisters Ignatius, Mary Ann, and Angela—went from Ohio to Miles City by train in early spring of 1884, some eight months before the Northern Cheyenne reservation was established. From Miles City they went by army ambulance in a small wagon train with a military escort from Fort Keogh, to a site seventy miles away on the Tongue River near present-day Ashland, Montana, twenty miles from Lame Deer. There, in a log cabin abandoned by its previous owner (who had papered its walls with pictures from *The Police Gazette*), the nuns set up a mission named for St. Benedict Joseph Labre of France. The soldiers unloaded the wagons, built an altar from rough boards, made a kitchen table and a few stools, repaired the stove, chopped firewood, carried water from the river, cleared a trail to the stream, brought hay from the nearest ranch for the nuns' bed ticks, and then returned to Fort Keogh. The missionaries were so short of furniture that for nearly two years one of the Sisters slept on a table or on the flat tops of trunks. But within their first week there they opened a school and began teaching Indian children English while the Sisters were learning to speak Cheyenne. Eighty years later the lights of St. Labre Mission were still shining on the banks of the Tongue.[3]

[3] The Ursuline Nuns were replaced at St. Labre Mission in 1933 by the school sisters of St. Francis. In 1965, five Capuchin Franciscan priests, two brothers, nine school sisters, and ten other staff members were carrying on the work begun in 1884. They were maintaining an elementary school, high school, and trade school, a health clinic, and a small industry, owned by an eastern enterprise, employing Indians as makers of plastic novelties—a pioneer venture in taking jobs to Indians on the reservations. The Northern Cheyennes, over the years,

It was September 1, 1890, before the government got around to building a school at Lame Deer. This was a log structure, twenty by forty feet, for fifty pupils. There were then, among the 865 Northern Cheyennes on the reservation, 204 of school age. St. Labre Mission was caring for sixty of them. Special Agent Walter Shirlaw, on an inspection tour in August, 1890, reported that the valleys of the Tongue River and Rosebud and Lame Deer creeks on the Cheyenne reservation were "very small when compared to those forming the arable lands of the Crow reservation . . . . The Cheyennes rank high morally and physically. There are fewer deaths than births. The women are chaste . . . . Industrial habits are not encouraged. [The Indians] really have nothing to do, but appear willing and anxious to do something. Drunkenness is unknown."[4]

Agency buildings in 1890 consisted of the agent's house and office, school, store buildings, a combined blacksmith shop and carpenter shop, a wagon shed and "stabling," and three buildings for employees. Shirlaw's report concluded: "The police force consists of six trusty Indians, with White Hawk as captain. The 'good' Indians are employed in government freighting for the agency; they also helped in erecting the agency buildings and twenty log huts for themselves. The rations issued are necessarily considerable on account of the many seasons of drought." (What the "bad" Indians were doing he didn't say.)

Mutual fear and suspicion between Indians and whites during the 1890's on several occasions magnified minor incidents into "Indian scares" which brought troops to the reservation for protection of panicky settlers. In December, 1891, the agent at Lame Deer telegraphed for soldiers, in fear of a fight over the impending arrest, by civil authorities, of an Indian named Walks Night, who was reported killing cattle off the reservation. The First Cavalry sent a detachment to the agency from Fort Custer,

also benefited from the religious and humanitarian efforts of representatives of other denominations, including the Mennonites, whose representative, the Reverend Rudolphe Petter, in addition to his missionary work, compiled a Cheyenne dictionary and grammar.

[4] Department of the Interior, Census Office, *Report on Indians Taxed . . . Eleventh Census*, 363.

and Brigadier General Wesley Merritt, commanding the Department of Dakota, with headquarters in St. Paul, Minnesota, ordered the commanding officer at Fort Keogh to establish a subpost at Lame Deer, which Company A, Twenty-second Infantry, under Captain John McA. Webster, promptly did—and named it Camp Wesley Merritt. Then word reached Fort Keogh that Walks Night was on his way to Keogh to surrender. A detachment of Cheyenne scouts intercepted him. When the whole story was unraveled, it came down to the fact that Walks Night had killed a heifer that broke into his feed lot and destroyed his hay.[5] Camp Wesley Merritt was maintained at Lame Deer for about ten years. It was manned by rotating detachments, usually in command of an officer but at times headed by a noncom.

In May, 1897, even greater excitement was aroused at Lame Deer over the killing of a white sheepherder named John Hoover. This time four cavalry troops and an infantry company were mobilized at Camp Wesley Merritt, when word reached Forts Keogh and Custer that settlers were fleeing to the safety of Miles City for fear of an Indian "outbreak" if the Indian suspected of the murder were arrested. Troops A and K, Tenth Cavalry, were dispatched to the scene from Fort Custer. They found the acting reservation agent, Captain George W. H. Stouch, Third Infantry, in conference with a group of citizens and four deputy sheriffs, and learned that the suspected slayer was a Cheyenne named Whirlwind, also known as Phillip Stanley. He was a member of White Bull's band. Captain Stouch thought it unwise to attempt the arrest of one Indian with only two cavalry troops, so Troop E of the Tenth came down from Fort Custer, and from Fort Keogh Troop A of the Eighth Cavalry and Company E of the Second Infantry converged on the scene. Major S. T. Norvell, Tenth Cavalry, took command of the little army at Camp Wesley Merritt.

The day that Major Norvell arrived, the suspected murderer, Whirlwind, was arrested without trouble by the acting agent and was turned over to the sheriff of Custer County under cav-

[5] Secretary of War, *Annual Report, 1892*, I, 115.

alry escort. Thereupon the settlers went home from Miles City; but "another stampede was created" (as the army report put it) among white persons living on Rosebud Creek by a report that two Indian accomplices would fight rather than submit to arrest. Again the fears were groundless; the cavalry took the suspects into custody without the firing of a shot or the raising of a voice, and turned them, too, over to the civil authorities.

This little drama dragged over a three-month period beginning in May. It was August 11 when the last of the troops returned to their stations and all was quiet again at Camp Wesley Merritt, with an officer and fifteen men left there to keep it so. The official report closed with the comment that "a careful investigation by Captain [Robert D.] Read, Tenth Cavalry, discloses the fact that there was no truth whatever in any of the reports which have appeared in newspapers as to hostile acts committed by Cheyenne Indians on or near the reservation." One white woman who wrote years later of her experiences in the exciting period at the time of the Whirlwind affair said that some of the white settlers in the area of Birney, a settlement twenty miles south of Lame Deer, fled as far as Sheridan, Wyoming, because of a rumor that the Indians were on the warpath and had wiped out a large number of whites.[6] She said "the truth of the matter was that Indians from all over the reservation were gathering at Lame Deer and asking protection . . . . They were just as frightened at the prospect of a war with the settlers as we were." And Whirlwind was never proved guilty of killing the sheepherder. In Miles City jail, awaiting trial, Whirlwind died of tuberculosis.

In 1900 the government enlarged the Northern Cheyenne reservation by moving its boundary ten miles east, to the Tongue River, making the total acreage 489,500. Here, over the years, the people of Dull Knife and Little Wolf have, haltingly at times, moved forward, although at late as 1965, when their numbers had increased to about two thousand, some of them were still existing in log huts with inadequate sanitary provisions and an unhealthful water supply. But more than a fourth of the

[6] Mrs. Grace Brewster-Arnold, Miles City *Daily Star*, May 24, 1934, Section Four, p. 7.

families were then self-supporting, and gradually the Cheyennes were learning to go the way the winds were blowing—to acquire, by their own efforts, with enlightened help, the better housing, the education, and primarily the motivation necessary to survive and progress in the world they had to live in. Their Tribal Council, formed in 1937 under the Indian Reorganization Act of 1936, was, with the aid of the Bureau of Indian Affairs, managing the tribal land so that it was a source of income. It was conducting a steer-branding enterprise that had thrived, failed, and was beginning to thrive again, and was preparing long-range plans for making the best possible use of a $4,300,000 judgment won in 1963 in the Court of Indian Claims for inadequate payment in the past for the land taken from the Cheyennes. There was a ray of hope ahead for "one of the bravest people who ever lived," as a fellow-Montanan described them in 1959.[7] The Northern Cheyennes were still traveling uphill, falteringly, at times, like the rest of us, and they still needed courage, but some of them still seemed to have it.

Between Indian scares, life at Fort Keogh in the 1890's had some of the gaiety that is associated with the decade. The regimental band kept on playing for dances, concerts, and theatricals which sometimes included minstrel shows. There were picnics, skating parties, card parties, and sports of many kinds. Service teams competed with each other and with civilian teams from Miles City in baseball, field events, and gymnastics, which included the swinging of Indian clubs and tugs of war on horseback. There were chapel services, singing groups, reading rooms, and a canteen for soldierly relaxation. Fraternal organizations thrived in the town, with memberships including service men from the post.

Christian Barthelmess was on detached service as photographer with the Indian Commission in late October, 1890, as his record shows. In January, 1892, he was sick in quarters with a service-incurred ailment, and in April he took a six months' furlough.

Toward the end of the decade, the United States, its domestic

[7] Joseph Kinsey Howard, *Montana: High, Wide, and Handsome*, 295.

borders assured, began to be involved in foreign affairs. Many lives changed course, including that of Christian Barthelmess, who was soon separated from home and family for the greater part of four years.

On February 15, 1898, the American battleship *Maine* was blown up in Havana Harbor, Cuba, and soon the United States, already stirred by the Cuban struggle for independence from Spanish rule, went to war to expel Spain from the island. The regular army, concentrated in the southern states, was built up from 28,183 officers and men to 58,688, plus 216,029 volunteers. While the navy swept the Spanish fleet from the seas, the army carried the fight inland at Santiago, Guantánamo, Siboney, and San Juan Hill, under the leadership of some of the graduates of the Indian wars—such officers as Nelson A. Miles, Henry W. Lawton, and Wesley Merritt—and the war was over by August 12. Cuba was freed, and the United States acquired Puerto Rico, Guam, and the Philippines. The army lost 290 officers and men killed, plus 2,565 dead from disease. The following year, American military forces turned their attention to the Philippines, where guerrilla warfare in behalf of Philippine independence continued until 1901.

As for Christian Barthelmess, his record shows he was in Cuba with the Second Infantry, June 24–August 10, 1898; was appointed sergeant March 18, 1899, at Camp Shipp, Alabama; returned to Cuba April 19, 1899; was discharged and re-enlisted (for three years) on December 1–2, 1899, at Powell Barracks, in the area of Cienfuegos, Cuba; was on furlough part of the next year but reached the Philippines October 1, 1900; was on detached service as guard of native prisoners of war February 6–15, 1901; was discharged and re-enlisted at Manila December 1–2, 1902, as principal musician, Second Infantry; was appointed chief musician from principal musician while at sea aboard the American transport *Sheridan* en route from Mariveles, Philippine Islands, to San Francisco June 3, 1903; applied, at Fort D. A. Russell, Wyoming, July 1, 1903, for retirement; was retired as chief musician, Second Infantry Band, July 17, 1903, and returned to his family and Fort Keogh.

Photographs taken by Barthelmess during the period of his foreign service were imprinted with his name and "2nd U.S. Infantry, Paso Caballo, Cienfuegos, Cuba," and "Cuartel de España, Manila, P.I."

The letter that Barthelmess sent through channels to the Adjutant General's Office at Washington, requesting retirement certified that his total actual service from his enlistment in 1876 to July 1, 1903, was twenty-six years and seven months; foreign service of three years, eight months, and three days added to this (foreign duty counted double) gave him an aggregate of thirty years, three months, and three days in the army.

So the Shadow Catcher laid aside his uniform—but not his black box. He kept on taking pictures, as he had done long before and throughout his service abroad. He was still the musician; he became conductor of a Miles City orchestra which played for occasions in the town. He took part in Masonic Lodge affairs, having become a Mason in 1900 at Cienfuegos, Cuba. He worked now and then at small jobs about the post, where the family continued to reside. He found time for reading, and built up a library, now in possession of his son Casey. It includes works on anthropology, history, primitive traditions and customs, myths, and languages. The library contained Plutarch's *Lives of Illustrious Men*, five volumes of the historical works of Hubert Howe Bancroft, eleven volumes of the *Annual Reports of the Bureau of American Ethnology*, Stoddard's three-volume edition of Washington Irving, and books on western military experiences, such as Colonel R. B. Marcy's *Thirty Years of Army Life on the Border* (1866) and Captain William F. Drannan's *Thirty-one Years on the Plains and in the Mountains* (1900).

That Barthelmess was a studious reader is evident from the many marginal annotations he made in his books. *The Ninth Annual Report of the Bureau of American Ethnology*, 1887–88, for example, contained an article on "The Medicine-Men of the Apache," by Captain John G. Bourke, Third Infantry. Some of Bourke's statements, and Barthelmess' penciled notations on the margins (indicated by italics), follow:

The Apaches will not let snakes be killed within the limits of a camp by their own people, but will not only allow a stranger to kill them, but will request him to do so. [BARTHELMESS: *The Navajos do the same.*]

The Apaches, when they kill a bear, don the bear skin and dance all night without a moment's cessation in the singing and dancing. [BARTHELMESS: *Saw one of these dances at Fort Bouwie, Arizona, 1881.*]

High up on the vertical face of the precipice of Taaiyalana [*sic*] there is a phallic shrine of the Zuni which I climbed with Mr. Frank Cushing. We found that the place had been visited by young brides who were desirous of becoming mothers. [BARTHELMESS: *Photographed it. Obceen pictographs.*]

Sandwich Islanders and Hottentots plaster their hair with lime made from burnt shells. [BARTHELMESS: *What is the matter of destroying insects?*]

In writing of the description of the Snake Dance of the Moquis of Arizona, I ventured to advance the surmise that the corn flour with which the sacred snakes were covered, and with which the air was whitened, would be found upon investigation to be closely related to the crithomancy or divination by grains of cereals, as practiced by the ancient Greeks. [BARTHELMESS: *Bosh!*]

Civilian though he now was, Barthelmess was not yet through with army life, nor with the job of reporting and recording it with his camera. In October, 1903, the War Department concentrated some nine thousand troops at historic Fort Riley, Kansas, for two weeks of intensive field maneuvers. Barthelmess accompanied the troops from Fort Keogh and returned home with a splendid series of photographs depicting the war games.

On the morning of April 10, 1906, Barthelmess sent his fifteen-year-old son Casey to collect some photography bills owed by post personnel. Casey collected what he could, and that noon placed the money in his father's hands. That was the last time Casey saw his father alive.

Barthelmess had taken a job helping to dig a nine-foot-deep sewer trench at the Fort Keogh hospital. At quitting time, while Barthelmess was still in the trench, preparing to climb out and go home, the engineer in charge of the job came along and stopped to talk about the work. Suddenly the sides of the excavation caved in. Barthelmess was completely covered, the earth level being four or five inches over his head. As swiftly as possible his face was uncovered. Then the ground was dug away until ropes could be fastened under his arms and he was dragged out and laid on the ground. Asked how he felt, he replied "All right," and a moment later he died.

"He was a fine old character," remarked the *Yellowstone Journal* of Miles City, April 11, "one for whom none could entertain sentiments other than respect, which deepened to affection on closer acquaintance."

The funeral was a military one, with Yellowstone Masonic Lodge No. 26 of Miles City participating. Then, in the post cemetery, the Shadow Catcher went to his long rest.

That autumn a flurry of excitement swept over parts of the Northern Plains, as embers break into flames again after a prairie fire. In this last Indian scare, Fort Keogh played a minor role. Three hundred White River Utes of the Uinta Valley reservation in northeastern Utah started on an unauthorized trip to South Dakota, where they had been told food was more plentiful than it then was in their own country. They traveled by foot, with a few wagons and some old-time travois. They were armed, and killed considerable game as they made their way across Wyoming. Cavalry troops converged upon them from several directions without provoking a fight. Fort Keogh's part in this campaign, as the War Department designated it, was to send a wagon train of rations and grain to Ashland, Montana, to supply cavalry from Fort Robinson, Nebraska. Two Sixth Cavalry troops from Keogh, under Captain George P. White, escorted the train. The restless Utes were talked into spending the winter in camp on the Fort Meade military reservation in western South Dakota; the next year they were quartered on the Cheyenne River Sioux reservation, and in the summer of 1908 they were back home in Utah.[8]

[8] War Department, *Annual Reports, 1907* (10 vols.), III, 70–73 and 123–25; also the reports for 1908 (9 vols.), III, 107, 108.

Fort Keogh's usefulness as a military garrison was steadily diminishing. The War Department's *Annual Report* for 1907 noted that Fort Washakie, Wyoming, had been abandoned May 1 that year, and that Forts Keogh and Assiniboine, Montana, were "in process of abandonment." General Orders No. 112, May 23, 1907, ordered most of the Fort Keogh garrison to the Philippines. Troops L and M, Sixth Cavalry, which stayed behind, were later transferred to Portland, Oregon, and the last detachments at Fort Keogh were relieved by Special Orders No. 146, Department of Dakota, October 27, 1908.[9] The barracks and mess halls, officers' quarters and parade ground were silent, except as a small caretaking detachment went about its work.

But again the winds of change fanned the embers, and in 1909 the post experienced a rekindling of usefulness—as the Fort Keogh Remount Depot. Instead of training men, it became a center for the buying and training of horses. The army had for years been buying its horses on the open market. Production of suitable mounts in adequate numbers began to decline in the early 1900's in New England and the middle eastern states which had been the main source of supply. The remount system was then devised and put into effect with establishment of the first depot at Fort Reno, Oklahoma, the second one at Fort Keogh in 1909, and the third at Front Royal, Virginia. The depots bought young horses from breeders in their immediate areas and conditioned and trained them for issue to the cavalry, artillery, and engineers. The motor age was developing swiftly among the country's civilian population, but had not yet changed the army.

Range horses bred on the ranch lands surrounding Fort Keogh made good cavalry mounts, and by 1912 Keogh was the largest supplier. Keogh had 794 animals on hand July 1, 1911; it received 867 during the fiscal year ending June 30, 1912, and from this total of 1,661 horses it issued 426 for cavalry use, 271 for artillery, and 110 for riding, sold 12 to officers and lost 53 by death, so that it entered the next year with 789 horses on hand,

[9] National Archives, Records Group 98. Records of United States Army Commands (Army Posts).

compared with 513 at Fort Reno, and 396 at Front Royal. By 1916, Fort Keogh's production was up to 1,773.

Old structures at Keogh were repainted, electric lighting was installed, steam heat was provided in the officers' quarters, and four electric machines for grooming horses were put in. By 1917, forage for the animals was being grown on 45,000 acres of the military reservation. The pasture was fenced and a 2,300-foot windbreak protected the stock.

The war in Europe brought horse buyers from the Allied armies to Miles City to purchase thousands of animals to ship abroad. During the Mexican crisis and the National Guard call-up that preceded America's entering the war, 55,000 horses were purchased in a three-month period for General Pershing's troops on the border. Auxiliary remount depots were established at Fort Bliss and Fort Sam Houston, Texas. But range horses from the Northern Plains were "more and more appreciated," said one army report, and were showing steady improvement in type, breeding, and appearance.

The Mexican crisis passed. National Guard units returning to their stations left a surplus of 40,000 army horses on the border. Declaration of war with Germany soon followed, and then the army called for 43,305 horses for the cavalry, 102,345 for light artillery, and 2,771 for heavy artillery, as well as 99,820 mules—wheel, lead, and pack. The Remount Service mushroomed, with auxiliary depots in many parts of the country and in theaters of war abroad. After the 1918 armistice, surplus animals numbering 170,355 were sold at public auctions for $19,073,544.36, or 60 per cent of cost.[10]

For a few years more after that, there was a need for army horses, but not much. That era was over. Military planning turned to motorization and aviation. The Remount Service faded, Fort Keogh fell silent again. Still, in 1965, almost eighty-nine years after the first tent stake was driven for Post No. 1, Cantonment on Tongue River, the once New Fort on Elk River in its second reincarnation was filling a civilian function in its

[10] This account of the Fort Keogh Remount Depot is based upon War Department, *Annual Reports, 1907*, III, 70; *1912*, I, 552; *1916*, I, 390; *1917*, I, 318, and *1919*, I, 747, 751.

The Miniconjou Sioux leader, Lame Deer, who was killed by soldiers on May 7, 1877, when he tried to shoot Col. Miles, was buried in this sandstone cave near the town and the stream named after him—Lame Deer. George B. Grinnell's account of the Lame Deer fight (*The Fighting Cheyennes*, 392) says that Lame Deer was scalped by White Bull, one of Miles's scouts.

General Nelson A. Miles in council with Northern Cheyenne chiefs at Lame Deer. Miles sits partly in the shadow, elbow on table. Christian Barthelmess in 1904 dated this photograph as having been taken in 1889. The Cheyenne Two Moon sits in the shade, exposing an expanse of white shirt front. On his left is James Rowland. Lt. Casey shows faintly back of Two Moon.

Cheyenne chiefs at the Lame Deer Council: Sits in the Night, Red Cherries, Brave Wolf, Two Moon, American Horse, Buffalo Hump, Spotted Wolf, and Old Wolf.

Early photograph of Lame Deer, agency for the Northern Cheyennes, established in 1884 some eighty miles southwest of Fort Keogh. Just left of center, in the distance, is a long shedlike structure used as a meeting place for Indian councils.

Indians (and James Rowland, in white shirt, who married a Cheyenne) wait in line for the beef issue—and through the doorway some of them watch the slaughtering.

Indians dancing at Lame Deer. With such a dance as this, the Cheyennes in 1884 welcomed the Ursuline nuns when they came by army wagon to found St. Labre Mission.

Omaha Dance of the Northern Cheyennes.

Whirlwind, one of Casey's scouts, in Cheyenne attire, before he got into trouble.

Whirlwind in the hands of the law, 1897, accused of murdering a white sheepherder. He died before he was brought to trial. In this photograph, taken at the Miles City courthouse, Whirlwind is handcuffed to Billy Smith, a local law officer. Right, a United States marshal; rear, Judge Gibb.

The original Ashland, located below St. Labre Mission, which is faintly seen in the distance, across Tongue River. This photograph, which was among those left by Christian Barthelmess, is stamped with the name R. C. Morrison, a Miles City photographer who sometimes assisted Barthelmess; it is likely that Morrison took this Ashland picture.

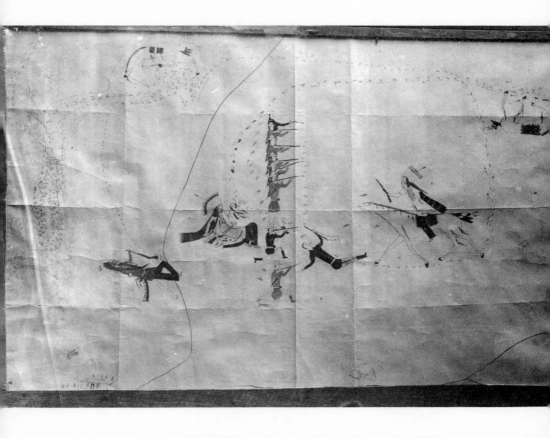

A Cheyenne drawing, artist and owner unknown, identified by Barthelmess as "Indian description of the killing of two Cheyennes by U. S. soldiers at Lame Deer in 1890." The incident was the dramatic suicide in September, 1890, of two young Indians, Headchief and Young Mule, who were "wanted" as suspects in the killing of whites and who sent word that on a certain day they would come in fighting. Troops drawn up to meet them shot them down as they charged down the hill.

Second Infantry officer group, Cienfuegos, Cuba, 1899. Identifications as supplied to Casey Barthelmess by E. H. Muir, later commanding general, District of Panama: Left, rear, civilian postmaster, then 2nd Lt. R. H. Wescott, 1st Lt. W. O. Johnson, Capt. P. E. Marquay, Maj. C. A. Dempsey, commanding; 1st Lt. Preston Brown, Capt. E. H. Muir, adjutant; Maj. A. H. Bowman, Contract Surgeon A. L. Simonton; front, 1st Lt. J. L. Hines, Capt. H. H. Benham, 2nd Lt. B. H. Watkins, 1st Lt. D. Baker, surgeon; 2nd Lt. J. G. Workizer, 2nd Lt. J. E. Bell, 1st Lt. A. E. Williams. Most of these men had served at Fort Keogh.

William Howard Taft, governor of the Philippines, rides through Manila streets, 1901, in the shade of an umbrella.

"The gallant Second to the front," Fort Riley maneuvers, 1903.

General Kline, Col. Gardner, and the Twenty-first Infantry cross a pontoon bridge on their way to camp after the last review, ending the 1903 maneuvers at Fort Riley, Kan.

Old Soldier Barthelmess, Second Infantry, Cuba, 1899, borrows a Second Cavalry horse to have his picture taken—perhaps recalling his first army days in 1876 as a Sixth Cavalry trooper and the time in 1886 when he rode from Fort Lewis, Colo., to the Grand Canyon and back on an army mule.

few remaining buildings. There, under the aegis of the Department of Agriculture's Range Livestock Experiment Station, a corps of experts went about their study of feeding levels, performance measures, and heritability estimates—to produce, not trained soldiers, nor cavalry horses, but better beef cattle. Miles City and environs were no longer Indian territory, but they were still cow country. Sentimentalists might wonder if this was old Fort Keogh's "Last Stand," but one thing about its future was sure: It would be remembered as long as America remembered its western frontier adventure.

A voice from that past came, many years after the death of Chief Musician Christian Barthelmess, to Casey E. Barthelmess of Miles City, the "Son of the Picture Man." It was the voice of former Trooper Ed. King, who had served at Fort Keogh, 1905–1907. From his home in Sacramento, California, in 1951, King wrote to Casey:

". . . I knew your father well, and I happened to be passing by when the accident that killed him occurred. I remember something happened inside me, a deep sorrow, to learn that a man so well liked was so abruptly gone. We felt so helpless . . . . I spent two years and four months at Keogh. It was there I first saw an Indian, first saw a man die, first learned to ride and shoot and swear, and thrilled at the feeling of companionship when I realized that I was a full-fledged cavalryman—that I belonged! I was not a praying lad, but sometimes I said a prayer, and I remember that I did so the day your father died. The last time my wife and I took a vacation, something drew me back along the old trail, and so we drove through Montana and past old Fort Keogh. I took my hat off when we reached there, and got out of the car and stood a long time alone. My wife did not break the silence. I just looked across the plains and imagined that I heard horses snorting the dust from their nostrils. I was sure I saw men riding by in column of twos, and heard bugles. Would you believe it, Casey, I caught myself reaching in my left shirt pocket for Bull Durham and papers, and getting ready to roll a cigaret, as I had not done then for forty years. Then my wife said, 'So this is it,' and I said 'Yep,' and we drove on."

--◄{ 137 }►--

Bibliography

MANUSCRIPTS

Fort Keogh documents, 1876–92, in the Casey E. Barthelmess Collection, Miles City, Montana.

Gray, John S. "Photographic Strays and Mavericks." Chicago, 1964. MS in author's possession.

Lincoln, Lewis A. Untitled MS in Library, State Historical Society of Colorado. Denver, 1964.

Nance, Judy. "Old Fort Keogh." Miles City, Montana, 1962. MS in Casey E. Barthelmess Collection, Miles City.

The Norris Papers, Huntington Library, San Marino, California.

Swaine, Charles S. "Memoirs of My Father and Mother" [Col. and Mrs. Peter T. Swaine]. N.p., 1937. MS in possession of Wallace S. Wiggins, Whittier, California.

GOVERNMENT DOCUMENTS AND PUBLICATIONS

American Military History, 1607–1958. Washington, Government Printing Office, 1959 (ROTC Manual No. 145–20).

Army Almanac: A Book of Facts Concerning the Army of the United States. Washington, Government Printing Office, 1950. Prepared at the Armed Forces Information School, formerly the Army Information School. Contains material current as of October, 1948, on the U.S. Army since its establishment.

Army Information Digest: The Official Magazine of the Department of the Army. Edited by Lt. Col. John S. Chesebro. Published under supervision of the Army Chief of Information. Washington, Government Printing Office, September, 1963.

Chronological List of Actions, &c., with Indians, from January 1, 1866, to January; 1891 [sic]. Office Memoranda, Adjutant General's Office.

Department of the Interior, Census Office. *Report on Indians Taxed and Indians Not Taxed in the United States (Except Alaska) at* the Eleventh Census: 1890. Washington, Government Printing Office, 1894.

————, Office of Indian Affairs. *Indians in the War.* Chicago, 1945.

Heitman, Francis B. *Historical Register and Dictionary of the United States Army, From Its Organization, September 29, 1789, to March 2, 1903.* 2 vols. Washington, Government Printing Office, 1903.

Hershler, N. *The Soldier's Hand-Book. For the Use of the Enlisted Men of the Army.* Washington, Government Printing Office, 1884.

Hodge, Frederick Webb. *Handbook of American Indians North of Mexico. Bulletin 30* of the Bureau of American Ethnology. 2 vols. Washington, Government Printing Office, 1907.

Indian Affairs, Commissioner of. *Annual Reports.*

Mooney, James. *The Ghost-Dance Religion and the Sioux Outbreak of 1890.* In *Fourteenth Annual Report of the Bureau of American Ethnology to the Secretary of the Smithsonian Institution, 1892–93.* Washington, Government Printing Office, 1896.

National Archives. Records of the Office of the Adjutant General, Records Group 94, Regimental Returns 22nd Infantry, 1887; Adjutant General's Office, Records Group 98; Register of Letters Received, 1887, Department of Missouri, Fort Leavenworth.

Smithsonian Institution. *Tenth Annual Report, 1855.*

Twenty-second Annual Reunion of the Association of the Graduates of the United States Military Academy at West Point, New York, June 12th, 1891. Saginaw, Mich., 1891. (Obituary of Edward W. Casey, No. 2501, Class of 1873, pp. 47–49.)

War Department. *Regulations of the Army of the United States and General Orders in Force on the 17th of February, 1881.* Washington, Government Printing Office, 1881.

War Department, Secretary of War. *Annual Reports.*

NEWSPAPERS

Der Westen, Chicago, Illinois.
Miles City Daily Star, Miles City, Montana.
Stockgrowers Journal, Miles City, Montana.
Yellowstone Journal, Miles City, Montana.

BOOKS

Abbott, E. C., and Helen Huntington Smith. *We Pointed Them North: Recollections of a Cowpuncher.* New York, Farrar and Rinehart, 1939. (Reprinted 1955 by the University of Oklahoma Press.)

Brown, Mark H., and W. R. Felton. *The Frontier Years: L. A. Huffman, Photographer of the Plains.* New York, Henry Holt and Company, 1955.

Burlingame, Merrill G., and K. Ross Toole. *A History of Montana.* New York, Lewis Historical Publishing Co., 1957.

Carter, Lt. Col. W. H. *From Yorktown to Santiago with the Sixth U.S. Cavalry.* Baltimore, Lord Baltimore Press, 1900.

Clarke, W. B. *Dusting Off the Old Ones.* Miles City, Montana, n.d.

Custer, Gen. George Armstrong. *My Life on the Plains; or, Personal Experiences with Indians.* Norman, University of Oklahoma Press, 1962. (A reprint, with introduction and annotations by Edgar I. Stewart, of the original book published in 1874.)

Dellenbaugh, Frederick S. *A Canyon Voyage: The Narrative of the Second Powell Expedition down the Green-Colorado River from Wyoming, and the Explorations on Land, in the Years 1871 and 1872.* New Haven, Yale University Press, 1926. (First edition was published in 1908 by G. P. Putnam's Sons.) Contains on p. 222 "Canyon of the Little Colorado, photograph by C. Barthelmess."

Denver Westerners' Brand Book: IX. Maurice Frink, editor. Denver, The Westerners, 1954.

Dustin, Fred. *The Custer Tragedy.* Ann Arbor, Mich., Edwards Brothers, 1939.

Eastman, Elaine Goodale, *Pratt, the Red Man's Moses.* Norman, University of Oklahoma Press, 1935.

Fergusson, Erna. *New Mexico: A Pageant of Three Peoples.* New York, Alfred A. Knopf, 1951.

Finerty, John F. *War-Path and Bivouac, or the Conquest of the Sioux.* Chicago, 1890. (Reprinted 1961 by the University of Oklahoma Press, with an introduction by Oliver Knight.)

Fletcher, Robert H. *Free Grass to Fences: The Montana Cattle Range Story.* New York, University Publishers, Inc., 1960. Published for the Historical Society of Montana.

Ganoe, William Addleman, Major of Infantry, U.S.A. *The History of the United States Army.* New York, D. Appleton and Company, 1924.

Grinnell, George Bird. *The Cheyenne Indians: Their History and Way of Life.* 2 vols. New Haven, Yale University Press, 1923.

———. *The Fighting Cheyennes.* Norman, University of Oklahoma Press, 1956. (Originally published New York, Charles Scribner's Sons, 1915.)

Hanson, Joseph Mills. *The Conquest of the Missouri, Being the Story of the Life and Exploits of Captain Grant Marsh.* New York, Murray Hill, 1946.

Howard, Joseph Kinsey. *Montana, High, Wide, and Handsome.* New Haven, Yale University Press, 1959.

Hurt, Wesley R., and William E. Lass. *Frontier Photographer: Stanley J. Morrow's Dakota Years.* University of South Dakota and University of Nebraska Press, 1956.

Hyde, George E. *Red Cloud's Folk: A History of the Oglala Sioux Indians.* Norman, University of Oklahoma Press, 1937.

———. *A Sioux Chronicle.* Norman, University of Oklahoma Press, 1956.

Johnson, Virginia Weisel. *The Unregimented General: A Biography of Nelson A. Miles.* Boston, Houghton Mifflin Company, 1962.

Kluckhohn, Clyde. *Mirror for Man: A Survey of Human Behavior and Social Attitudes.* New York, McGraw-Hill Book Company, 1949.

Kuhlman, Charles. *Legend Into History: The Custer Mystery.* Harrisburg, Pa., The Stackpole Company, 1951.

La Farge, Oliver, with the assistance of Arthur N. Morgan. *Santa Fe: The Autobiography of a Western Town.* Foreword by Paul Horgan. Norman, University of Oklahoma Press, 1959.

La Guardia, Fiorello H. *The Making of an Insurgent, an Autobiography, 1882–1919.* Philadelphia, J. B. Lippincott Company, 1948.

Lummis, Charles F. *Mesa, Canyon, and Pueblo: Our Wonderland of the Southwest.* New York, The Century Company, 1925.

Marquis, Thomas B. *Wooden Leg, a Warrior Who Fought Custer.* Lincoln, University of Nebraska Press, n.d. (Reprinted from the original edition, 1931, *A Warrior Who Fought Custer.*)

Matthews, Washington. *Navaho Legends Collected and Translated by Washington Matthews, M.D., LL.D., Major U.S. Army, ex-President of the American Folk-Lore Society, with Introduction, Notes, Illustrations, Texts, Interlinear Translations, and Melodies.* New York and Boston, published for the American Folk-Lore Society by Houghton, Mifflin and Company, 1897. Vol. V of *Memoirs of the American Folk-Lore Society.*

Miles, Nelson Appleton. *Personal Recollections and Observations.* Chicago and New York, The Werner Company, 1897.

Monaghan, Jay. *Custer: The Life of General George Armstrong Custer.* Boston, Little, Brown and Company, 1959.

————. *The Book of the American West.* New York, Julian Messner, 1963.

National Park Service, U.S. Department of the Interior. *Soldier and Brave: Indian and Military Affairs in the Trans-Mississippi West, Including a Guide to Historic Sites and Landmarks.* Introduction by Ray Allen Billington. Vol. XII, "The National Survey of Historic Sites and Buildings." New York, Harper and Row, 1963.

O'Connor, Richard. *Black Jack Pershing.* Garden City, N.Y., Doubleday, 1961.

Pride, W. F., Captain of Cavalry U.S.A. *The History of Fort Riley.* Topeka, Capper Publications, 1926.

Remington, Frederic. *Pony Tracks.* New York, Harper and Brothers, 1895.

Rickey, Don, Jr. *Forty Miles a Day on Beans and Hay: The Enlisted Soldier Fighting the Indian Wars.* Norman, University of Oklahoma Press, 1963.

Sandoz, Mari. *Crazy Horse, the Strange Man of the Oglalas.* New York, Alfred A. Knopf, 1942.

————. *Cheyenne Autumn.* New York, McGraw-Hill Book Company, 1953.

————. *Horse Catcher.* Philadelphia, Westminster Press, 1957.

————. *Hostiles and Friendlies: Selected Short Writings.* Lincoln, University of Nebraska Press, 1959.

Schmitt, Martin F., and Dee Brown. *Fighting Indians of the West.* New York, Charles Scribner's Sons, 1948.

Simpson, James H. *Navaho Expedition: Journal of a Military Reconnaissance from Santa Fe, New Mexico, to the Navaho Country Made in 1849 by Lieutenant James H. Simpson.* Edited and annotated by Frank McNitt. Norman, University of Oklahoma Press, 1964.

Spaulding, Oliver Lyman. *The United States Army in War and Peace.* New York, G. P. Putnam's Sons, 1937.

Summerhayes, Martha. *Vanished Arizona: Recollections of My Army Life.* Edited by Milo Milton Quaife. Chicago, Lakeside Press, 1939. (Originally published in Philadelphia in 1908.)

Taft, Robert. *Photography and the American Scene: A Social History, 1839–1889.* New York, The Macmillan Company. 1938.

Tompkins, Col. Frank. *Chasing Villa: The Story Behind the Story of Pershing's Expedition Into Mexico.* Harrisburg, Pa., The Military Publishing Company, 1934.

Bibliography

Underhill, Ruth M. *The Navajos*. Norman, University of Oklahoma Press, 1956.

Utley, Robert M. *The Last Days of the Sioux Nation*. New Haven and London, Yale University Press, 1963.

Waters, Frank. *Masked Gods: Navaho and Pueblo Ceremonialism*. Albuquerque, University of New Mexico Press, 1950.

White, William Carter. *A History of Military Music in America*. New York, Exposition Press, 1944.

PERIODICALS

The American Anthropologist. Washington, D. C.

Arizona and the West: A Quarterly Journal of History. Tucson, University of Arizona Press.

The Colorado Magazine. Denver, State Historical Society of Colorado. Published quarterly.

Journal of American Folk-Lore. New York, New York.

Montana: The Magazine of Western History. Helena, Montana Historical Society.

Montana State College Farmer. Bozeman, Montana.

Montana Farmer-Stockman. Great Falls, Montana.

The Race of Sorrows. Published every three months at Ashland, Montana, by the St. Labre Mission, Father Emmett, ed.

The Westerners Brand Book. Issued monthly as the official publication of the Chicago Corral of the Westerners.

Winners of the West: Official Publication of the National Indian War Veterans of the U.S.A. "Published in the Interest of the Survivors of the Indian Wars and the Old Army of the Plains." St. Joseph, Missouri.

Index

Index